THE KINGDOM OF FORGIVENESS

THE KINGDOM OF FORGIVENESS

The freedom of accepting
and practising God's
unconditional forgiveness

GERALD O'MAHONY

kevin mayhew

kevin
mayhew

First published in Great Britain in 2019 by Kevin Mayhew Ltd
Buxhall, Stowmarket, Suffolk IP14 3BW
Tel: +44 (0) 1449 737978 Fax: +44 (0) 1449 737834
E-mail: info@kevinmayhew.com

www.kevinmayhew.com

© Copyright 2019 Gerald O'Mahony

The right of Gerald O'Mahony to be identified as the author of this work
has been asserted by him in accordance with the Copyright, Designs and
Patents Act 1988. The publishers wish to thank all those who have given their
permission to reproduce copyright material in this publication.

Scripture quotations are taken from The New Revised Standard Version
Bible: Anglicised Edition, copyright © 1989, 1995, Division of Christian
Education of the National Council of the Churches of Christ in the United
States of America. Used by permission. All rights reserved.

Excerpts from the English translation of The Roman Missal © 2010,
International Commission on English in the Liturgy Corporation.
All rights reserved.

All rights reserved. No part of this publication may be reproduced, stored in
a retrieval system, or transmitted, in any form or by any means, electronic,
mechanical, photocopying, recording, or otherwise, without the prior written
permission of the publisher.

9 8 7 6 5 4 3 2 1 0

ISBN 978 1 84867 989 4
Catalogue No. 1501610

Cover design by Rob Mortonson
© Image used under licence from Shutterstock Inc.
Edited by Linda Ottewell
Typeset by Angela Selfe

Printed and bound in Great Britain

Contents

About the author	6
Introduction	7
1. Conditional forgiveness, then and now	15
2. The freedom of not judging – and Jesus	23
3. Jesus forgives before asking for improvement	31
4. The Lord's Prayer, two versions, and 'Abba'	39
5. 'Abba' for Jesus, then for us – beloved children	45
6. Two sides of the gospel: faith guarantees security	51
7. Kingdom of 'Pay what you owe' or 'Forgive'?	59
8. Bread, water and wine: 'wine' and the Word	67
9. Sacrifice and forgiveness	73
10. Mothers and fathers	79
11. Why Jesus had to die	85
12. What only God can do	91
13. All sins are forgiven	99
Epilogue	103
The Key to the Kingdom	105

About the author

Gerald O'Mahony was born in Wigan, Lancashire, and at the age of 18 joined the Society of Jesus (the Jesuits). He was ordained priest at the age of 30 and was a school teacher for four years. Then, after 10 years as an advisor to teachers of religion, he worked for 30 years with the team of retreat givers at Loyola Hall Jesuit Spirituality Centre, near Liverpool. Nowadays, Gerald lives in semi-retirement at St Wilfrid's Presbytery in Preston, Lancashire.

Gerald has written 27 books on spirituality, always to make God's love better known and understood. He is still, and always has been, urgent about the importance of forgiveness. *The Kingdom of Forgiveness*, book 28, builds on the theme of his very first book – forgiveness, God's forgiveness as the basis of ours.

Introduction

This little book is about unconditional forgiveness, holding that God's forgiveness is unconditional and is there from eternity into eternity. That is not what I was taught as a child, but it is what I now, at the age of 84, believe without reservation. Moreover, God wants us to forgive one another without conditions, because selective forgiveness is ineffectual towards bringing peace on earth, and revenge is murderous.

Unconditional forgiveness is the theme of these pages, and here I wish to introduce the progress of the argument in the following chapters. Think, if you will, of this book as a jigsaw puzzle, and here are the outside pieces already found and giving the structure to what follows. The chapters below will fill out the picture, as jigsaw pieces do.

I shall begin with the traditional conditional forgiveness often ascribed to God in the Old Testament: 'If you do as I say, says God, you will prosper and possess the land I promised. But if you break my laws there will be serious trouble, and that will be the end of our relationship.' Words like these are frequently to be found, and they imply, 'I will not forgive you.' Such an attitude attributed to God is also a common attitude between humans of any age and time: 'Please me, and I will be content; I might even be pleasant to you in return. But harm me enough or often enough and I will never forgive you, unless perhaps you apologise and make it up to me. I might not even forgive you then, being too deeply hurt.'

Next, when Jesus tells us, 'Do not judge, and you will not be judged', he is not speaking anything specifically religious. His words there are also words of wisdom for the present time, they are not particularly aimed at escaping judgement after death; they are words that can bring peace of mind all through life. The words can be hugely helpful for anybody who acts on them, whether or not they believe in Jesus as someone divine, and whether or not they practise any religion at all.

My third chapter will point out something not often noticed, namely that Jesus always forgives before he expects the forgiven one to start living a better life. Instead of 'Behave yourself from now on and I will forgive you for what you did in the past', Jesus acts the other way round: 'You are forgiven for what you did: now try and do better in future.' Extraordinary!

The fourth chapter looks at the Lord's Prayer in the two versions given in the Gospel of Matthew and in the Gospel of Luke. Thanks to the study of Joachim Jeremias[1] I can understand that Luke's version (Luke 11:2-4) is most likely the original as spoken by Jesus, and the Matthew version which we normally use (Matthew 6:9-13) has small but important additions put there by the Apostles from other vital sayings of Jesus. For me,

---

1. *The Central Message of the New Testament*, Joachim Jeremias, SCM Press, 1965.

the most important conclusion is that Jesus taught his disciples to call God 'my Father', 'Abba', when praying on their own. 'Our Father' belongs when we pray along with other children of God.

Fifthly, what has 'Abba, Father' got to do with forgiveness and unconditional forgiveness? Jesus was the first person in the history of the human race to call the supreme God, 'Abba'. In giving us our prayer to pray as he does, saying, 'Abba, my Father', he is giving us disciples an adoptive form of his own relationship with God. Once God is 'my Father' and I am baptised as beloved son or daughter of God, then God's love is that of a parent. God loves me before, while or after I sin, and forgives accordingly. God did not learn to forgive only when we became sinners.

Sixthly: The two sides of the gospel. Such is the theme of a book I wrote many years ago, entitled *The Two-Edged Gospel*[2], in which I noted how many of the gospel images have an active and a passive side. The most obvious is that we are (on the one side) sheep of God's flock and (on the other side) called to be shepherds of one another. Fundamentally, we are children of God, yet called upon not to cling to the privilege but to act as if we are only servants – as Jesus did. And so on, through a dozen or more images.

Where this two-sidedness helps towards understanding unconditional forgiveness, is that all the passive images

---

2. Published by Eagle 1995 and by Gracewing 2005.

(sheep, child, guided etc.) do not depend on how active we may or may not have been. I may admittedly have been a poor specimen of a shepherd in my life, but I am still one of the sheep of the flock, for whom Jesus gave his life. There is cause for gratitude.

In the seventh chapter I face the fact that Jesus does not always seem to 'forgive first, look for improvement only afterwards'. His strictures of the Pharisees, the Sadducees and the scribes are pretty blunt, and right up to the last minutes of his life he does not appear to offer them much in the way of forgiveness. The prophets of old often thunder the anger of God; Jesus, Son of God, is sometimes pictured as getting angry. How then can I hold that God is forgiveness, and that God is always forgiving? How can the visionary Julian of Norwich say so clearly that God is never angry?[3] What is this, then, about 'never getting out of prison till you have paid the last penny' (Matthew 18:34)? What is the result of choosing 'Pay up what you own me!' as my god, as the kingdom I wish to inhabit? There is a kingdom of forgive, and there is a kingdom of pay up.

The eighth chapter is about the symbolism of bread, water and wine as used in the Eucharist. The bread, when it is taken up, is used as a sign of the human body of Christ. The water signifies his human life and the wine signifies his divine life. 'Body, soul and spirit' is the way St Paul describes the three (1 Thessalonians 5:23).

---

3. Revelations of Divine Love, 46 and 49.

A small prayer then asks that as the water is mixed with the wine, so Jesus' divine life became one with his human life; then, we pray, may our human life become one with his divine life. The wine comes from outside to be one with our bread-and-water selves, the gift of divine life we pray to come from outside to lift up our human body and its life.

How are we to identify this divine life in ourselves? What is the wine from outside if not the ability to call God 'Abba'? To us who receive the body, the human life and the divine life of Jesus in the Eucharist, the exchange leads to our calling God 'Abba', and therefore leads also to the forgiveness of our sins as God's beloved children.

The ninth chapter wants to say something about sacrifice. God does not need placating or appeasing by sacrifice; indeed God does not need placating or appeasing at all. The Church over the centuries has been very insistent that what Jesus did on the cross was a sacrifice, and in the Mass we celebrate that same sacrifice. How can this truth be upheld without picturing God as forgiving on conditions? Is there not another sense in which the cross of Jesus can be seen as a sacrifice, and in which God's will is still the motivating force? Jesus sacrificed his life to uphold the constant forgiveness of his Father. Where too is the likeness between the sacrifice of his son by Abraham, and what Jesus did in obedience to his Father?

The tenth chapter deals with God as Father, not Mother. 'Mother' is us; we humans are the mothers in Jesus' scheme of things. We may all be mothers of Jesus when we are penetrated by the love of God from outside, but we can never be fathers of Jesus. Here, ultimately, is the reason why Jesus speaks as God as 'He' rather than 'She'. We are not promised a hundredfold of fathers for the one sire we gave up for his sake, but there is no limit to the number of mothers. Incidentally, I do not think Jesus ever asks his Abba for mercy for us, but he does ask for our forgiveness. 'Abba, have mercy on me' would sound somewhat strange, whereas 'Abba, please forgive me' sounds normal.

Chapter eleven says why Jesus had to die. Jesus insisted that God has already forgiven us – 'Your sins are forgiven'. He knew this because he knew God as his 'Abba', his own Father. The enemies Jesus made were adamant that God had forgiven them, but not anybody else. There were things you had to do, to be forgiven by God, and only they had done the necessary things. Jesus' way of forgiving sinners first, before asking them to change their life, was anathema to his enemies. So, he had to go. Yes, it was his Father's wish that he should die. Jesus died, rather than deny God's unearned forgiveness. Everybody had to be told that God is Abba, even if Jesus was going to be crucified in the attempt to shut him up. Jesus on the cross said, 'Father, forgive them; they do not know what they are doing.' He really did say that. They were unwilling to receive forgiveness as a gift. They treated forgiveness as something you earned.

The twelfth chapter is about the resurrection of Jesus. Twenty-eight out of thirty times the New Testament asserts that God raised Jesus from the dead, not that Jesus raised himself. The apostolic writers knew from experience that only God could do such a marvel; and the fact that this was the work of God showed Jesus was vindicated. The accounts of the resurrection appearances differ in some details, but there is a kernel of agreement about the reality of the event, and the total change in the hearts and lives of the believers. Life is now lived in consolation, not only by Jews but by Gentiles as well.

The thirteenth chapter holds that all sins are forgiven already, past, present and to come, and that this truth is ultimately what Jesus died for. He was killed, executed, for holding it. Usually we have to empty our heads of many prejudices in order to see the central truth in the words and actions of Jesus, but sometimes this total forgiveness is spelled out clearly: 'since all sins have been forgiven, there is no longer need for (Temple) sacrifices for sin'; 'go and tell them the news that they are reconciled' (Hebrews 10:18 and 2 Corinthians 5:11–6:2). They are reconciled already, before you reach them, but they do not know it yet. So tell them.

Then there is the article of faith from the Apostles' Creed: I believe in the forgiveness of sins. Not just my sins, not just your sins, but everybody's sins.

Conditional forgiveness, then and now

To start with, a few examples of what I would call conditional forgiveness, or conditional love, from the Old Testament. They are not the whole story of the Old Testament, but they tend to be the sort of passages that stick in people's memories and imaginations. How could anyone think of God's love and forgiveness as unconditional, given the number of times the Bible shows God saying 'if' or 'unless'?

Here, accordingly, is a sentence from the Book of Exodus: 'Now therefore, if you obey my voice and keep my covenant, you shall be my treasured possession out of all the peoples (Exodus 19:5). God was there reminding Moses, at Mount Sinai, of how the people had been rescued from Egypt 'on eagles' wings'. For the future, provided they hear God's voice, all will be well.

The next quotation not only says 'if', but threatens terror 'if not'. Again, this is God instructing Moses in the Law. 'If you follow my statutes and keep my commandments and observe them faithfully . . . you shall . . . live securely in your land. I will . . . be your God, and you shall be my people. But if you will not obey me, and do not observe all these commandments . . . I in turn . . . will bring terror on you' (Leviticus 26:3-5, 12, 14-16).

The beautiful chapter in Deuteronomy about loving God above all things includes the following verse: '. . . keep all his decrees and his commandments that I [Moses] am commanding you, so that your days may be long' (Deuteronomy 6:2). The 'if' there is implied rather than voiced. Further along in the same book, a threat is clear: '"Cursed be anyone who does not uphold the words of this law by observing them." All the people shall say, "Amen!"' (Deuteronomy 27:26).

In his old age Joshua, the leader who followed after Moses, warned the people that the success they had achieved might not last: 'But just as all the good things that the Lord your God promised concerning you have been fulfilled for you, so the Lord will bring upon you all the bad things, until he has destroyed you from this good land that the Lord your God has given you. If you transgress the covenant of the Lord your God, which he enjoined on you, and go and serve other gods and bow down to them, then the anger of the Lord will be kindled against you, and you shall perish quickly from the good land that he has given to you' (Joshua 23:15, 16).

Next, think of King Solomon, son of King David. In Solomon's reign the prosperity of Israel was at its height. The Lord appeared to Solomon and said to him, with other things: 'As for you, if you will walk before me, as David your father walked, with integrity of heart and uprightness, doing according to all that I have commanded you, and keeping my statutes and my ordinances, then I will establish your royal throne over

Israel for ever, as I promised your father David ... If you turn aside from following me, you or your children, and do not keep my commandments and my statutes that I have set before you ... then I will cut Israel off from the land that I have given them; and the house that I have consecrated for my name I will cast out of my sight' (1 Kings 9:4-7).

God's covenant with David (as related in 2 Samuel chapter 7) was to establish the throne and the royal house of David for ever. Now in the case of Solomon the element of uncertainty reappears, though historically we believe, as Christians, that the throne of David did and does last forever in Christ Jesus.

One more example of 'if' might be quoted, though many more examples of conditional love and forgiveness may be found in the words of the Old Testament. In the poems of the book of Sirach comes the promise:

> Be a father to orphans,
>   and be like a husband to their mother;
> you will then be like a son of the Most High,
>   and he will love you more than does your mother.
> (Sirach 4:10)

These examples of conditional love and forgiveness on God's part are, of course, not the whole story from the Old Testament. There are a lot of promises attributed to God which do not have any conditions attached. For instance, very early on in the Bible, Abraham is promised by God that his descendants will one day number as many as the stars in heaven (Genesis 15:5) or the grains of sand on the seashore (Genesis 22:17), and that he would become a great nation (Genesis 12:1-3). Admittedly, Abraham had first to get up and go in search of his promised land, but the promise held good, even when Abraham was old and still had no son, and even when he had been willing to sacrifice his one and only son Isaac, if that was what God wanted. The promise about having many descendants held firm from beginning to end.

From a Christian point of view, there are several other promises of God included in the annals of the Old Testament, promises of a Messiah who would one day come. Whatever the conduct of the people or their leaders, a final leader would come to set the record straight. Thus, for instance, there would come a shepherd of the people who would depose the shepherds who were mistreating the sheep of God's pasture instead of minding them. God would look after the sheep himself, he or his son David (though King David had already died) – see Ezekiel chapter 24.

Again, as was mentioned above, there was a promise that there would always, for all time, be a king of David's line to rule the people (2 Samuel 7:8-16). For a Christian, this promise is fulfilled in Jesus, son of David and King risen from death, and the sinfulness of the original King David did not alter the promise.

Then there was a promise made long ago by Moses speaking for God, that though he, Moses, was dying, his people should not be alarmed: God would raise up a prophet like Moses from among their brethren, who would speak to them all that God commanded – to him they would listen (see Deuteronomy18:15-18). In the time of Jesus, people were still asking when this prophet would come (John 1:21), and the vision of Jesus at the Transfiguration shared with Peter, James and John confirmed to the Apostles that Jesus was that very prophet (Matthew 17:5; Acts 3:22).

Another promise freely given is that of the Son of Man in the seventh chapter of the Book of Daniel. The immediate contemporary reaction was to identify this victorious leader with the people as a whole, but then when the Maccabees were ousted by the armies of the Roman Empire, the search was still on for a leader like that (Daniel 7:1-28). Christians see that prophesy as being fulfilled in Jesus, in spite of Roman domination continuing in his lifetime (see Mark 8:27-29).

Another strange line in a psalm turns out to have been a prophesy for Christians in Jesus, and there are no conditions attached: 'For you [the Lord] will not abandon my soul to Hades, or let your Holy One experience corruption (Acts 2:27, quoting Psalm 16).

It does seem as though the later prophets had seen so many times that God relented and wanted the people to start all over again amid the ruins of past disasters. 'The Lord is merciful and gracious, slow to anger and abounding in steadfast love' (Psalm 103:8). The temple once destroyed would be rebuilt, the city walls of Jerusalem would be rebuilt. There would be a new covenant, one that dwells in the heart rather than in the books (e.g. Jeremiah 31:31-34). After all, 'I have loved you with an everlasting love' (Jeremiah 31:3), so the new covenant will be an eternal covenant (Ezekiel 37:26) which will mean their having a heart of flesh, not a heart of stone (Ezekiel 11:14-21).

These great prophets still did not put one image on the coming everlasting covenant. Perhaps Jeremiah came the closest to what Jesus would bring: Jeremiah has God saying, 'I have loved you with an everlasting love' and everlasting love goes back in time as well as forwards. It means, 'I have always loved you, and I always will.'

Still there remains from the books of the Old Testament a picture of God setting up a conditional kingdom, then the people breaking the conditions, then the ensuing disaster. Then we have God sending one more prophet to stand among the ruins, exhorting everyone to try again, because God has relented. The disasters were real, and the rebuilding difficult.

Even with Christian believers there can still be the same, or a similar pattern. We have our moral standards, and in times of temptation or of difficult decisions, we are inclined to think of God as a judge of great power, who can cause havoc with our lives if we break the rules. Not even that thought is enough always to make us do the right, but difficult thing. We tend to forget how Jesus taught clearly enough that sickness (John 9:1-3) or disasters (Luke 13:1-5) are not God's way of punishing us for sinful behaviour. They happen anyway, and God's everlasting love is present throughout. It is not true that God will love us less if we do the wrong thing: everlasting means everlasting.

Nonetheless, as a human race, regardless of whether we believe in God, we tend to harbour hurts and be slow to forgive completely. This is true at a family level, it is true at a community level, it is true at a national or international level. For those of us who aspire to be imitators of God, it is of considerable importance whether we think of God as one who forgives unconditionally. Otherwise we could argue that, like God, we are not called on to forgive those who break the moral rules.

What are we to think about those Old Testament prophets who claim to express the anger of God? Given that they or their successors also express the forgiveness of God for disobedience, is it possible to wonder whether this is the anger of the prophet rather than the anger of God? A mother driven to distraction by her children in a giddy mood might say, 'Just wait till your father comes home! He will be very, very cross'; whereas when the father does come home he does not show any anger.

Thus far is only the first of thirteen chapters about the forgiveness of God. We will be returning to fill in the picture.

The freedom of not judging – and Jesus

When Jesus tells us, 'Do not judge, and you will not be judged', is that an example of conditional forgiveness, or could it be heralding unconditional forgiveness? Is he saying, 'If you do not judge others, then as a consequence you yourself will not be judged'? Or is Jesus saying, 'You yourself are forgiven already, but you will never experience forgiveness as long as you carry on judging other people'? That way round leaves God's forgiveness without conditions.

Some people in authority have to judge, like magistrates and judges, parents and teachers. They are right to have standards and to uphold them: but in judging whether another did right or did wrong, they are surely, as Followers of the Way of Jesus, bound to separate the deed from the doer. So-and-So did wrong, but I am still obliged to separate what they did from the person who did it. In the end the judge, parent or teacher does not know the inmost heart of the perpetrator; and in any case for Jesus, the perpetrator is to be forgiven. Restraint or even prison may be called for, but still Jesus wants forgiveness.

Which brings us on to other sayings of Jesus, commands really. How many times does he expect us to forgive one another? Peter, the spokesman, one time asked Jesus that question. He asked, is to forgive seven times enough to satisfy Jesus? Jesus replied, not seven times, Peter, but seventy-seven times (some others recollect his saying seventy times seven times!). In other words, the right thing to do is to forgive friend or enemy every single time. Now that may seem to be a tall order for a mere mortal, but of course Jesus would not ask us to do anything that God does not already do. So therefore God has the fixed intention and good will to forgive me every single time I fail in my duty. In another exchange Jesus says to forgive your brother or sister seven times in the day if they say they are sorry (see Luke 17:3, 4). The seventy times seven passage did not even say the offender has to say sorry (see Matthew 18:21, 22).

Jesus expects us to love our enemies and to forgive them (see Luke chapter 6 and Matthew chapter 5). 'Forgive, and you will be forgiven' (Luke 6:37). That saying could be understood as conditional forgiveness on God's part, or it could be that we are already forgiven by God but we will never see it unless we ourselves forgive our enemies. Jesus came and comes to open our eyes to see it, not to put conditions on God's forgiveness of us.

What about the sentence in the Lord's Prayer about forgiveness, 'Forgive us our sins, for we ourselves forgive everyone indebted to us' (Luke 11:4)? This is a prayer, saying we have already done what Jesus asked of us, namely we have let off everyone who was in debt to us; we ask for our own sins to be forgiven, which is not our right but which depends on God's desire to forgive. We are not asking for forgiveness as a right simply because we have done what we ought to do (compare Luke 17:16). The version of the Lord's Prayer most commonly used has '. . . and forgive us our trespasses, as we forgive those who trespass against us.' That would give us a kind of boomerang: the way we forgive them (or not) is the way we ask you to forgive us (or not) – which is decidedly uncomfortable and seems to leave God's unconditional forgiveness in doubt.

Sometimes people will say, 'Forgive? Yes, I can forgive and I do forgive. What I find hard is to forget.' Perhaps the way round that is to forgive all over again each time the painful memory comes to mind, seventy-seven times over every day, if necessary. Also, I have a particular thought that sometimes helps, regarding serious harms that have been done. The second letter of St Paul to Timothy advises Timothy to beware of Alexander the coppersmith, 'He has done us great harm.' For an apostle there seems to be a need for caution in dealing with the likes of this Alexander, even though he is presumably forgiven and prayed for (2 Timothy 4:14, 15).

'If anyone takes away your goods, do not ask for them again' (Luke 6:30). The presumption is, that this is the way God acts with us all the time. We take hold of the goods that God provides, and we use them, neglect them or squander them – like oil, or water. God does not ask for them back. We are strongly advised by Jesus to do the same for one another, and to be generous with things that are in short supply. 'Do good, and lend, expecting nothing in return. Your reward will be great, and you will be children of the Most High; for he is kind to the ungrateful and the wicked' (Luke 6:35). These actions, and the rewards, are based on a vision of God as endlessly forgiving.

The Sermon on the Mount in Matthew also warns about calling one another bad names, but there is a positive, forgiving message to be drawn from the passage (see Matthew 5:21-26) as well as the threats. Roughly speaking, what Jesus says is not to be angry with a brother or sister, or else you will be the one deserving to be judged; and if you insult a brother or a sister you will be the one deserving to be hauled before the council; and if you call someone else 'traitor' you will be the one deserving the death penalty. In other words, beware of calling other people names, because the names really refer to yourself rather than to the one you insult. The positive message is that God does not call us names, and does not want us as children of the Most High calling one another names. Every single child of God has the same right to a good and honourable name, for who we are, and regardless of what we have done or failed to do.

A parallel message can be found in Jesus' advice regarding the best place at table when there is a banquet or a wedding breakfast. If you go to the top place, you are sure to be toppled, whereas the lowest place is safe, nobody else will want it. We are all equal as children of God, and wisdom dictates that we wait to be shown our perfect place by God (see Luke 14:7-11 and Mark 10:40).

A major parable of Jesus again poses the question as to whether Jesus thinks of God's forgiveness as unconditional. The parable is that of the Unforgiving Debtor (Matthew 18:23-35). A king settling his accounts with his slaves finds one who owes him ten thousand talents, a sum like billions of pounds sterling today. The man could not pay, and was about to be imprisoned and all his family sold. The king listened to the debtor's pleas for mercy, and let him off. What did the man do next but throttle another slave who owed him only hundreds, threatening to have him thrown into prison. When the king got to hear of this he was disgusted, and changed his mind about letting the man off for his debt of billions. That, says Jesus, is how his heavenly Father will treat us unless we forgive one another.

Is that behaviour of the king in the story compatible with what I am holding true, that God forgives us unconditionally? For sure, the difference between the two sums of money in the story is significant. As I read the parable and reflect on its meaning for me, it seems to be saying that I was let off an enormous sum compared with the relatively tiny sum which I was meanly trying to claw back. I can see that the debt I owe God for sun, moon, stars, earth, history, family, friends, existence, loving care, personal gifts etc. etc.

is completely unpayable – God does not ask payment. The debts owed to me are tiny by comparison.

But can it not be that the same is true here as it was in the matter of not judging? God gives the billions of gifts all the time and with no conditions, but if I will not forgive relatively small matters then I blind myself to the goodness of God, which is effectively withdrawn from me. God does not change his mind according to my behaviour: it is as though there are two kingdoms, the kingdom of forgiveness and the kingdom of pay-what-you-owe, and what the man in the parable did was to choose the wrong kingdom. The kingdom of forgiveness is, however, still there: always was, is, always will be. To take my own case again, if I carry on being unforgiving to others, the huge gifts of God (the sun, moon, stars etc.) are a debt and a burden on my conscience, whereas if I forgive everyone else then the gifts of God are gifts, and I do not have to pay for them.

Jesus tells us, when we give a luncheon or a dinner party, to invite the poor, the crippled, the lame and the blind, because they cannot pay us back (Luke 14:12-14). Once again Jesus is giving us a picture of God as someone who gives and gives but does not request payment. There is no question of 'I give you these things provided you pay me back.' There are no conditions. In common decency, if we find ourselves in a situation where we can pay something back, as by helping the poor, the crippled, the lame and the blind, then that is a small way towards paying the unpayable. But God's generosity is not limited by our weakness.

One saying of Jesus that I keep coming back to is this: 'Whatever you ask for in prayer, believe that you have received it, and it will be yours' (Mark 11:24). Surely, if that saying refers to anything at all, it must refer to God's forgiveness? First, to pray and ask for forgiveness; second, to believe that I already have that forgiveness. In other words, the forgiveness was already there before ever I asked for it. Similarly, then, when Jesus says, 'Ask, and it will be given to you; search, and you will find; knock, and the door will be opened for you' (Luke 11:9), the implication is that what I ask is already there for me, what I am looking for is not hidden, and the door is not locked, but is left open for me, when I wish to enter God's presence. So, forgiveness is there for the asking, forgiveness is not being withheld from me, and the door is already open for this sinner. For 'sinner' read 'child of God' and the picture makes sense.

Jesus forgives before asking for improvement

The average group of religious worshippers anywhere in the world will usually expect anyone who wants to join them to first of all give up evil ways. Then, in consequence, the sinners will be forgiven and they will be allowed in. Jesus has a different way of bringing people to lead a good life: he starts by forgiving. Then he waits to see a change in behaviour for the better. There are many examples of this manoeuvre of his in the Gospels, and it brought him hostility and detestation from certain quarters of society right from the outset of his public life.

Take, for example, the charming, touching story of the man who was let down through the roof because there was no longer room at the door for four friends, stretcher and paralysed man to come in to Jesus (see Mark 2:1-12). This happened in Capernaum, apparently when Jesus came back to the house of Simon's mother-in-law after an absence of some days – it was very early in Jesus' public ministry. Mark tells us that Jesus saw the faith of the four stretcher-bearers, and said to the paralytic, 'Son, your sins are forgiven' (verse 5). Then he added, 'I say to you, stand up, take your mat and go to your home' (verse 11). And that was just what the man did.

Jesus' critics on this occasion were correct in saying that only God can forgive sins, and in fact Jesus said the same: 'Son, your sins are forgiven' is the polite Jewish way of saying, 'Son, your sins have been forgiven by God.' But the hostile listeners were still outraged at Jesus claiming to know God had forgiven the man's sins – the patient was a paralytic, which must mean that sin was the cause of the deformity, or so they reasoned. The man had not been through any healing ceremony or made sacrificial offerings for his sins. Jesus was simply telling him not to let the thought of his past sins paralyse him any more: the future was open to him again. 'God has forgiven your sins, whatever they were.'

Jesus said the same precious words to a woman who was a sinner: 'Your sins are forgiven' (Luke 7:48). To his critics on this occasion Jesus said, 'I tell you, her sins, which were many, have been forgiven; hence she has shown great love' (Luke 7:47). Because her many sins were forgiven, that was why she was showing such gratitude and affection: she was bathing Jesus' feet with her tears and drying them with her hair; then she was kissing his feet and anointing them. She was thanking Jesus for telling her that God had forgiven her everything, and Jesus said her faith in him had saved her – she could go in peace. It was not the case that Jesus saw how sorry she was, and therefore forgave her: her love was out of gratitude that Jesus had declared her to be already forgiven by God.

A very clear example of Jesus' manoeuvre with sinners is the case of Zacchaeus (see Luke 19:1-10). Zacchaeus was the little man who climbed a sycamore tree to get a better look at Jesus passing by. Jesus the Prophet from God (so it was thought) looked up at Zacchaeus, told him to climb down and to get ready a meal at his house to welcome Jesus. That was the prophet overlooking all Zacchaeus' meanness and extortion as a chief tax-collector and instead offering friendship. This time Jesus did not say, 'Your sins are forgiven', but his actions amounted to an offering of God's forgiveness.

Zacchaeus jumped at the chance, and halfway through the meal he responded handsomely to Jesus' offer: he promised to pay back four times the amount to anyone he had defrauded, and to give half his money (he was rich) to the poor. Now if Jesus, looking up at Zacchaeus in the tree, had said, 'Zacchaeus, if you promise in future to keep all the Law of Moses to the letter, I will come to your house for a meal', Zacchaeus would not have been impressed. What is more, if Jesus had said, 'Zacchaeus, if you give half your money to the poor, and if you promise to pay back four times the amount to anyone you have defrauded', then Zacchaeus would have run a mile from the sycamore tree.

The woman at the well (see John 4:1-42) had had five husbands and was living with a man who was not her husband. It seems likely that she came to the well alone at noon to avoid being shunned by other women coming early to the well. Jesus asks her for a drink of water, and then gets into a serious conversation on many religious topics. He lets her know that he is aware of her marital history, but does not let that stop him from taking her seriously. To all intents and purposes, he is treating her as forgiven, and he is openly admitting to being the Messiah, the Christ. As a result the woman left her water-jar and went to fetch the people of the city – a forgiven ambassador.

Even the manic-depressive man in Mark's Gospel (Mark 5:1-20), the one with the Legion of demons inside him, is not condemned. Jesus restores him to calmness, and when the man, now cured, asks to come away in the boat with Jesus and the twelve, the answer is no, but instead a different mission is entrusted to him: to go home to his friends, and to tell them how much the Lord has done for him, and what mercy he has shown him.

John's Gospel has another clear example of Jesus' forgiveness, or rather of his declaration of forgiveness: the woman who had been caught in adultery (John 8:2-11). When none of the men around in the temple claimed to be without sin and hence no one was about to throw a stone at her, they went away and left Jesus alone with her. No one had condemned her any longer, and Jesus said, 'Neither do I condemn you. Go your way, and from now on do not sin again' (verse 11). As if to say, God has forgiven your sin, and will forgive you seventy-seven times over if need be, but please, from now on be grateful, and do not do this again.

I think the forgiveness of Peter is another clear example. At a turning point in Jesus' training of his chosen disciples, Peter is inspired to realise Jesus is the Christ (see, for example, Matthew 16:13-18). At that moment Jesus calls Simon 'a rock', recognising that Simon was here inspired by God. Thus Simon gets the name Peter, 'the rock'. Yet we know how unlike a rock Peter's behaviour continued to be – boastful always, then treacherous when Jesus was on trial. Peter the great leader completely denied that he had ever known the man Jesus – but then broke down and wept bitterly when he saw what he had done. Yet Jesus forgave Peter so gently, telling him to feed the sheep and the lambs . . . and it was at that moment that Peter became truly, and for ever, the Rock. God's choice of Peter still held, and Jesus went along with that choice wholeheartedly.

All the disciples and apostles benefited by being chosen and forgiven, women as well as men. Levi, son of Alphaeus, was sitting at the tax booth by the lake when Jesus said, 'Follow me' (see Mark 2:13, 14). Whatever customs-style booth Levi had been working at, now suddenly the Rabbi is saying, 'It's all right. Don't worry about the past: come with me.' Sinners and tax-collectors at table with Jesus were able to see themselves as welcomed back by God (see Mark 2:15-17). Many became disciples.

Martha, who welcomed Jesus into her house, must have wondered what she was doing wrong when Jesus her guest praised her sister Mary ahead of her (see Luke 10:41, 42). But in the story of the raising of Lazarus from the dead, Martha has a starring part, so Jesus obviously did not hold anything against her for not having understood his promptings (see John 11:27).

The condemned criminal crucified beside Jesus did not condemn him and was, in turn, not condemned in the eyes of Jesus: 'Truly I tell you, today you will be with me in Paradise' (Luke 23:43). Even Judas, who betrayed Jesus with a kiss, was still called 'Friend' by Jesus (Matthew 26:50), though he came with a large crowd from the chief priests and the elders of the people to arrest Jesus. Judas did at least repent later of what he had done (see Matthew 27:3).

The same theme, of forgiveness first but then followed by improvement to a better life, comes in some of the stories made up and told by Jesus. At first sight the Prodigal Son in Jesus' wonderful parable, seems to have sinned first, then come to repent of what he had been doing (see Luke 15:11-32). He made his way home, determined to admit to his father that he had sinned 'against heaven and against you, Father', and to ask for a position as a common slave rather than to be reinstated as younger son. Instead, the father will hear nothing about his son becoming a slave: he calls for the best robe, for a ring for his son's finger and sandals for his feet. He has the choice calf killed for a feast, a feast with music and dancing.

Two details at least, if not more than two, point to the father's forgiveness coming before the prodigal's sinful life, not just after. The father saw the returning sorry figure of his son 'while he was still far off' (verse 20), which strongly suggests the father was out looking up the road every day in the hope that his son might one day reappear. The other detail in the telling is that the father did not walk, but *ran* to embrace the wanderer. Also, the father cut off the prepared speech when the son was trying to suggest he was no longer fit to be called 'your son'. The father's love and forgiveness instead dated from the day the baby boy was born, and had never been withdrawn.

On a more modest scale, the story of the lost sheep has something of the same impact (see Luke 15:1-7). A man has a hundred sheep and loses one of them. He searches high and low, and when he finds the lost one he rejoices more than he ever did over the ninety-nine others. This is a parable from the same chapter of Luke's Gospel as that of the returning son, and what it is teaching is that Jesus comes looking for the lost ones, the sick and the sinners, not for the found and healthy ones.

Now this may seem to be a rather enormous jump, but I am sure that the fact Jesus was without sin (2 Corinthians 5:21) has a vital link with the truth that his heavenly Father loved him completely from before the foundation of the world (John 17:24). Surely, forgiveness did not begin in God, along with love, only when human beings were created and began to sin. The Father's love must always have included a guarantee that 'I will love you, my Son, whether or not you will love me in return', otherwise the love would have been conditional. Because the love was unconditional from before the beginning of time, Jesus never took up the option of sinning. There is the basis of the New Covenant introduced by Jesus, which says in effect, 'I will be true to you, even if you are untrue to me.' The hope is, 'You will be true.'

The Lord's Prayer, two versions, and 'Abba'

The first version of the Lord's Prayer is startling to read, for anyone familiar with the version used in services in most Christian worship. The version that startles reads like this, 'When you pray, say:

> Father, hallowed be your name.
> > Your kingdom come.
> > Give us each day our daily bread.
> > And forgive us our sins,
> > > for we ourselves forgive everyone indebted to us.
> >
> > And do not bring us to the time of trial.'

(Luke 11:2-4)

Compared with the words our tongues are more used to saying, there seem to be some items missing. Should it not be 'Our Father', rather than just 'Father'? Is the Father not still 'in heaven'? And why is such a vital prayer as 'Your will be done on earth, as it is in heaven', left out? And all very well about not being put to the test, but should we not pray also to be delivered from evil, or from the evil one? Comparing the version in Luke's Gospel, above, with Matthew's version (Matthew 6:9-13) or the words most commonly used in worship, there seem to be some very important prayers left out by Luke.

Joachim Jeremias, in the classic little book referred to in the Introduction, argues convincingly that Luke's version is the original version as taught by Jesus, whereas the version in Matthew has very important elements included by the Apostles after the death and resurrection of Jesus. When we pray on our own, 'Father' is the proper way to address God, but when we pray along with other disciples then 'Our Father' is best, since God is not my Father exclusively but is Father to all of us disciples.

The apostles Peter, James and John were close enough to Jesus when he prayed in the Garden of Gethsemane on his last night, to hear him pray hour after hour, 'Abba, Father, for you all things are possible; remove this cup from me; yet, not what I want, but what you want' (Mark 14:36). That must surely be why the apostles would feel bound to put the same prayer in with the rest of Jesus' model prayer: 'Your will be done on earth as it is in heaven.'

As for 'rescue us from the evil one' or 'deliver us from evil', could it not be that the apostles had prayed, but had not prayed seriously enough, not to be brought to the time of trial (lead us not into temptation), so now they see the need to pray for rescue as well?

A rabbi would only have one version of his master prayer for his disciples to keep as a model, so (argues Jeremias) which of the two came first, Luke's version or Matthew's version? Did Luke and his associates decide that Matthew's version was unnecessarily long, and drop the bit about 'Our', the bit about 'Your will' and the bit about 'rescue' on their own authority? Or was Luke's version the one Jesus taught as his prayer, and the apostles after the events of the first Easter saw the need to add a few words? All things considered, Luke's version has to be the one first taught in that form by Jesus himself.

For me, with my desire to clarify God's forgiveness as being unconditional, the key word in the comparison of both versions of the Lord's Prayer is: 'Father', just 'Father', not 'Our Father'. When asked by one of his disciples to please teach us how to pray, Jesus said to that one disciple, 'Pray like this: "Father, hallowed be your name".' He gave to that disciple and to all of us disciples the opening to call on God as 'my Father'. Mark gave us not only Jesus addressing God as 'Father', but also gave us the original Aramaic word *Abba* used by Jesus, rather than just the Greek translation of it. *Abba*, in its own language, is a familiar form of address from a secure child to a loving male parent. As such it is the first, and up till then, the only time in the history of language that the word was used by one human being speaking to God in prayer. Yet here was Jesus telling each of his disciples to pray using the same word.

The word 'Abba' goes along with its regular translation 'Father' in two key places in the letters of the apostle Paul. In his letter to the Galatians Paul writes, 'And because you are children, God has sent the Spirit of his Son into our hearts, crying "Abba! Father!"' (Galatians 4:6).

In Paul's letter to the Romans we have, 'When we cry, "Abba! Father!" it is that very Spirit bearing witness with our spirit that we are children of God' (Romans 8:15).

Jesus just naturally (for him) prayed to God as his own Father, as he always had (compare Luke 2:49). In the early version of the prayer he taught his disciples, he is sharing his so-far unique relationship to God with his disciples as his adoptive brothers and sisters. There is a one-to-one element in Jesus' way of prayer which he shares with us, and that element tends to be sidelined by the combined prayer of the Church. Yet if ever I find myself isolated from my brothers and sisters, I can still call on God as my Father.

One of the greatest prophecies of the Christ in Isaiah tells of God declaring, 'Here is my servant, whom I uphold, my chosen, in whom my soul delights' (Isaiah 42:1). This prophecy is echoed by the voice that came from heaven at the baptism of Jesus: 'You are my Son, the Beloved; with you I am well pleased' (Mark 1:11). Along with Jesus, those baptised are not only sons and daughters of God, but beloved sons and daughters of God, not only as a family but also one by one. Thus I can say to God, 'I am your beloved son' or 'I am your beloved daughter'.

We are also children, over and above being servants. The great Old Testament prophets like Isaiah, Jeremiah and Ezekiel could sense that something more was to be expected from God, but they did not put a word to it. That word came to be 'Abba', spoken by one man and then to be shared with all the world. A slave may be executed and no questions asked, a servant may be sacked for poor performance, but a son or a daughter will always, always get another chance. Jesus' story of the Prodigal Son, and the way the father always loved the son, is one and the same story with that of our adoption by God. Before Abraham was, Jesus is (John 8:58); and before the foundation of the world God chose us, his daughters and sons (Ephesians 1:4). Our relationship with God is not simply that each of us was created; in addition, we are sons and daughters, each of us loved with an everlasting love.

The word 'Abba' is not simply a child's word for a father, but is still used by the same person in adult years (compare Luke 15:21), just as today a familiar word like 'Daddy' may continue to be used when the child is no longer a child. We may need to re-enter childhood to feel comfortable with calling God 'Father' or 'Abba' or 'my Father' or by some name more personally familiar we had for God when we were children. For myself, that would be 'Holy God'. And hence, 'Abba, have mercy on me' sounds somewhat heavy. Children do not ask for mercy from their parents, though they do ask for forgiveness.

In recent years we Roman Catholics were asked to take on a new translation of the Roman Missal. The new one felt unfamiliar, but nonetheless it was following the Latin words the Church had been using for centuries. To introduce the Lord's Prayer, the new translation goes like this:

At the Saviour's command
and formed by divine teaching,
we dare to say: Our Father ...[4]

In the Latin, which was normal when I was first ordained, that runs:

Praeceptis salutaribus moniti
et divina institutione formati
audemus dicere: Pater noster ...

All I wish to say here, is that daring as it is to call God 'Our Father', it is infinitely more daring to cry 'Abba! *my* Father!' The Spirit who leads us to cry like that is our Advocate (John 14:16, 17), our lawyer for the defence, who knows the way to obtain forgiveness, no matter what we may have done or failed to do.

---

4. From the English translation of The Roman Missal.

'Abba' for Jesus, then for us – beloved children

There is an important little story in the Gospel of Matthew (17:24-27) which looks at first like a miracle story but is, in fact, a teaching story. The people collecting the temple tax ask Peter whether the Master usually pays the temple tax. Peter tells them, 'Yes, he does' but then goes to Jesus to ask if he said the right thing. Jesus then asks Peter whether the kings and rulers of this world demand taxes from their own children, or only from the ordinary citizens. Peter replies that surely a king would never impose taxes on his own children. Then Jesus points out that as he and Peter are God's children, the temple tax is not for them: he and Peter have no obligation to pay for the maintenance of their Father's house. But all the same, a voluntary contribution would be in order, so Jesus sent Peter fishing to raise the wherewithal to subscribe.

The lesson to be learned from this exchange is that God does not demand taxes of his children, that Peter, like Jesus, is one of the children, and what we do in service to God is in the nature of a voluntary contribution, now that we are children of God. The truth has set us free (compare John 8:32).

So, we are not slaves, we are free. There is no need to be put back into slavery by picturing God as anything but a Father to whom we are beloved. For a child of God, God is not a judge or a policeman or a tyrant. God is not the kind of person to trap us or trip us up. My Father is not observing every little thing I do so as to hold it against me if I get something wrong. When I have important decisions to make, God is telling me that I will still be his beloved daughter or son, even if I choose the option that turns out to have been a mistake.

Before God I need never to pretend to be other than I am. With human beings we often have to pretend, put on a good face, keep up with the crowd, give a good impression. But with God there is none of that: with my Father I can be completely honest and yet know that it is all right to be as I am; if I do wrong, there is always forgiveness. There is forgiveness before I do wrong, as I do wrong and likewise afterwards. There is no need to be a slave to what other people may be thinking. A good parent loves the weakest of the children, and would never despise a child for not being as bright as the others.

There is no need for despair, once I am the beloved child of God. My Father does not look for success. Jesus points the way, telling of the good shepherd who will leave the ninety-nine sheep just to go looking for the lost one. Anyone facing despair is of more concern and love to God the shepherd than the healthy who do not need such compassion. The Father does not look for success, but loves the also-rans as much as the star performers. No need to be a slave to Olympic ambitions, or to be top of the class.

No need to dither, whether to do this or that. Most times, just picture a sheep in front of a shepherd: she wonders, shall I go this way or that way? But if she goes this way, the shepherd will shield her with this hand, and if she goes that way, the shepherd will shield her with that hand.

No need for slavery to rules and regulations, short of the law of the land, maybe. Look at the way Jesus could break rules when there was a charitable need, such as when he often healed sufferers on a Sabbath day, although according to the religious rules of the time he should not have been doing that.

Being a child of God brings freedom, even from sin, in the sense that a sin committed is not a signal that all is lost, which is what sin tries to tell us. The knowledge that I am God's beloved son or daughter brings healing and forgiveness right away and enables me to start again, knowing that God has not given up on me. If we really understood God's everlasting love, we would never sin again, but that lesson takes a lot of learning.

'Who cares what people think of me!' Well, we all care about what people think, but the foundation for self-confidence is knowing that, as a first-generation child of God, I am as noble and high-born as anyone else on earth before me or after me. One prince or princess cannot be looked down on by any other prince or princess, especially when they are of the same family. 'My Father the King thinks the world of me, so I am not too bothered if you think otherwise.'

Another precious freedom that Jesus brings as my brother is the freedom from having to judge or fix other folk. There is something in most of us that likes to criticise those around us, to judge them and fix them and put them right. We do not immediately realise that to shed ourselves of the onus to fix other people is a freedom. When Jesus says, 'Do not judge', he is setting us free from a self-imposed duty we thought we had.

'Regrets' is another feature Jesus allows us to be free from. 'I wish I had done this and not that; I am sorry that such and such happened, when I made the wrong decision.' Jesus encourages us to live with what happened, rather than being dragged back or dragged down by wishing that yesterday had been different. God loves me now, not yesterday; I am God's child now, and now is too precious to submerge in regrets. There may be lessons to learn from the past, but please, no regrets.

Competition? Competition is all right when it brings out the best in people. Ultimately, though, we are all equally loved in the arms of God, and there is no blessing in sadness over not having won – the World Cup, the Eurovision Song Contest, the Number 1 song in the charts, the May Queen, the student popularity poll, the most applause in the show, the easiest talker in the family . . . whatever the competition. 'Nobody can be me better than I can, and God loves me.'

Praise is pleasant, and we all like to be praised. Praise is good for us, and every child needs praise. But as a child of God I do not need praise all the time: I can get by without it. As a follower of the Way of Jesus I will be called upon at times to love without being loved in return, and to give without always being appreciated. 'Love to be unknown, and to be counted for nothing' says Thomas à Kempis' *The Imitation of Christ*[5] and it will happen sometimes. Then we can fall back on being God's beloved: 'You are my beloved son, with you I am well pleased', or else 'You are my beloved daughter, with you I am well pleased.' Nobody else around may know that, but it is the truth.

Lastly, what about worrying over my own self-image? That worry can be quite taxing, but ultimately Jesus has provided the way not to worry about self-image. Once I know myself as a beloved son or beloved daughter of God, a God who does not judge me, then no better image could ever be found.

---

5. Book 1, Chapter 2, paragraph 3.

Two sides of the gospel: faith guarantees security

The last chapter gave us Jesus saying that God does not demand taxes from his own children, but that a voluntary contribution is very acceptable. This present chapter will develop the scope of voluntary contributions God would like to receive, as well as underlining the reality of our being children of God. 'Child of God' appears in many different images used by Jesus, under different titles.

A long time ago I noticed that there are two sides to many of the images used in the Gospels. I shall take them one by one, or rather, pair by pair. The first pair is 'sheep' and 'shepherd'. We are all of us sheep in God's flock; we can each of us be found in the lost sheep of the parables; we are comforted when Jesus speaks to the five thousand, because they are like sheep without a shepherd. Yet Jesus calls the sheep that is me to become a shepherd, to share in his work of caring for other people. Sheep do not grow into shepherds: there is a special grace or ability that Jesus provides as time goes by. Then I become a shepherd, perhaps a good one, perhaps a poor one. My contribution as a shepherd is voluntary, and I do the best I can. If my shepherding is poor, well, I am still and always one of God's sheep, and God will still love me. That I believe.

Next take 'enlightened' and 'light for others'. Another early Christian name for baptism was 'enlightenment'; the day of baptism was the day of realising oneself as daughter or son of God. For a time, that is enough, just to rejoice in being chosen. But then, in gratitude, comes the desire and the need to share my light with others, as it were to hold up my baptismal candle so that it gives light to everyone in the house. The light in the first place was a free gift of God; the holding it up for others to see, that is voluntary.

Jesus wants us to become like a 'child' so as later to be given 'power' from on high. In Britain we have lollipop ladies and lollipop men, local officials designated to hold up the traffic so that children can cross the main road safely on their way to or from school. These ladies and men have a staff or a standard shaped like a lollipop, such that every road user will recognise and respect. A child may not cross the road except under the care of the lollipop lady (or man). But a little child can be given the power, by the official, to take the hand of another even smaller child and cross the road when authorised. We take our orders from God, but if and when we voluntarily guide others, we do so only under God.

Next, consider the pairing of 'son/daughter' and 'servant'. Paul writing to the Philippians (Philippians 2:4-11) makes the link clear. Although Jesus was of divine nature, he did not cling to his divinity but emptied himself to become a servant. A baptised person is a sharer in the divine nature, and that is guaranteed. But a baptised son or daughter of God is invited to make a voluntary contribution by becoming a servant to others as Jesus was. There is no minimum or maximum: the amount and quality of service will stem from the awareness of gratitude in the heart of the daughter or son.

Another pair of images is 'built on rock' and 'rock for others'. As a child of God my position is guaranteed for ever. With the confidence which results from such security I can be a solid support to others who feel themselves to be on shifting sands.

Then take 'fish' and 'fisher'. A fish is a hallowed symbol of Christ, and as a symbol fits also any Christian. Peter and Andrew, James and John were fishermen, but they were also fished-for by Jesus and well and truly netted: they spent the rest of their lives with him, and as fishers for other people. Baptised I am a fish; confirmed I become a voluntary fisher.

In the Gospels there often come 'coins', and there are 'coin-seekers'. The most notable coin is the one with Caesar's image embossed upon it, and the coin-seekers include the housewife who lost a valuable coin, and the numerous tax-collectors who came to listen to Jesus and even to follow him. Now a coin does not have to do anything to become precious, all it needs is someone to want it. Each of us only has to believe that we are made in the image of God, and in gratitude to give ourselves back to God. Then too we may be called to go collecting other images of God into God's treasure house.

'Seed' and 'sower' is another clear two-sided image. I am the soil, God sows the seed in my field; then one day the seed in me grows and hopes for a harvest. There is no obligatory size of a harvest, each seed does its best. But the basic field or even vineyard is always there, loved by a hopeful God. The seed comes from God the sower, and represents the action of baptism: human soil, divine seed.

Jesus is our 'guide' on the Way, and our own basic truth is that we are 'guided', or otherwise we shall never find the destination. Having been guided, however, so as to understand the Way, we can become guides ourselves. Our baptism, if rightly understood, teaches us that we are children of God, whose guidance is not a tax, but an invitation to grow.

Another image, rather more hidden in the Gospels, is the picture of God 'waiting upon us'. In the parable of the unforgiving debtor the initial debt to the rich man is ten thousand talents. I have suggested above that such a huge sum brings to mind our debt to God, of the gifts of creation, of redemption and our own personal gifts. It sounds as if God, out of immense wealth, is laying it all before us: sun, moon, stars, earth, love, land, sea, sky, as if he were a waiter or a sales person. What it nudges me to do is to wait on my fellow beings by placing my gifts at their disposal.

The Baptism and Transfiguration of Jesus could be said to fall into the same 'twin' pattern. In the Baptism the voice from heaven says, 'You are my Son, the Beloved;

with you I am well pleased' (Luke 3:22). That is fixed, permanent, and given before Jesus had done anything very notable to deserve it. The voice from the cloud at the Transfiguration, on the other hand, repeats about the beloved Son, but this time is speaking to the three Apostles: 'This is my Son, the Beloved; listen to him!' (Mark 9:7). Jesus is being invited to speak out for who he is, as he spoke out his name when he was on trial.

In the same sort of way every Christian being baptised is fixed as a child of God, whether or not they have ever done anything at all to merit such a name. And in the Sacrament of Confirmation they are still God's beloved children but are now volunteering to speak out what they believe. Confirmation, to the best of my memory, has always been considered a voluntary sacrament.

Even in the signs of the Eucharist there is the same double: the gift and the invitation. The 'body of Christ' comes to me as perfect gift, all his love and his life, with no holding back. If I am the child of God, Jesus is my totally dedicated brother, asking for nothing but acceptance. The 'chalice' on the other hand has a voice that says, 'Can you drink the cup that I drink?' Drinking the cup is an offer to take whatever comes in his service, but is also an intoxication to help us do impossible things out of love.

'Water' as an image tends to go with baptism, with washing, with quenching thirst, whereas 'fire' goes with tongues, with Pentecost, with speaking out, with transfiguration.

All the starting images I have listed here, plus some more, are to do with faith: I am God's sheep or lamb, enlightened, a little child, God's daughter or son, built on rock, fish caught, coin with God's image, field sown with seed, guided on the Way, waited on by God, Jesus baptised, my baptism, bread of the Eucharist, water. These images are all free, they do not cost anything to believe. I need all of them, but they are free.

All the images on the other side are to do with love: shepherd, light for others, power, servant, rock for others, fisher, coin-seeker, sower, guide, waiter, transfiguration of Jesus, confirmation, chalice, fire. These are all costly, but they are voluntary.[6]

What has all this about the two sides of the gospel to do with God's unconditional forgiveness? Consider how all the passive images and the starting images tell us that if I do poorly or badly in the active images, I can still believe in God's everlasting love for me. I may be a poor sort of shepherd, but God still loves this lamb, no matter what. I may be a poor servant of God, but I am still God's beloved child.

Another feature of the Gospels is worth considering here in the context of the two sides of the gospel, namely 'merit'. It seems to me that Jesus wants us to aim for poverty in money, but equally for poverty in merit. By that I mean not taking to myself any merit for doing good, but instead disclaiming any praise or self-praise.

---

6. For a fuller enquiry into the two sides of the gospel, see *The Two-Edged Gospel – Gift and Invitation*, Gerald O'Mahony, Gracewing 2005.

Take, for example, the older brother of the Prodigal Son. He was very disgruntled at his father's welcome of the sinful son back home again. He felt that he himself had merited at least as much, if not more, of a fuss to be made of him, for he had worked hard in his father's field year after year. Jesus the storyteller does not agree: the father was right to give a big welcome to the sinner.

Again, the labourers in the vineyard who had worked hard all twelve hours were cross that those who had only worked for one hour should receive the same wage as themselves. Jesus, on the contrary, says that the owner of the vineyard (and God as well) is entitled to reward whoever he wishes with his riches.

The Pharisee praying in the temple despised the tax-collector who he supposed had not fulfilled anything like as many religious regulations as he himself had, but Jesus the storyteller reckons the humble tax-collector was the one who went home justified.

All in all, Jesus wants us to do good deeds, but never to count them. If they are too few, we get discouraged; if they are very many, we are liable to become big-headed, whereas in themselves good deeds are just as much a gift of God as being a child of God is a gift.

Heaven, and the living presence of God, is not something we merit, no matter how hard we try. Heaven is beyond us. We can try to merit heaven, so long as we know we are aiming beyond ourselves, and that in the end we will have to be picked up and carried into heaven like everybody else.

Kingdom of 'Pay what you owe' or 'Forgive'?

In the last chapter I was gathering pairs of gospel images, each one with a passive side and an active side, the passive side being guaranteed by God but the active side depending on a voluntary contribution from us human beings. There is, however, one further pair which has a different tone, namely 'forgive' and 'forgiving'. Yes, 'forgiven' is guaranteed by God, but 'forgive' is not voluntary, not optional, in God's eyes. In this chapter we can investigate the reasons why this pair of images is different from the others.

To go straight to the heart of the matter we need to return to the parable of the Prodigal Son. Here comes the sinful son, longed for and welcomed back by the father. Here also comes the elder brother, affronted that the father seems to give more time and affection to the sinner than to him, the faithful son. The elder brother refuses to go into the house and join in the celebrations; he refuses to forgive his younger brother. The father is faced with a dilemma: does he disown the sinner to please the elder brother, or does he persuade the elder brother to share in the welcome for the sinner? The father clearly has no intention of disowning the one he has just welcomed back with great delight; so the solution is up to the elder brother, either to forgive and join in, or to stay outside and cut himself off.

The introduction in Luke's Gospel to the chapter about the father and the two sons runs like this: 'Now all the tax-collectors and sinners were coming near to listen to Jesus. And the Pharisees and the scribes were grumbling and saying, "This fellow welcomes sinners and eats with them"' (Luke 15:1, 2). This was the reason why Jesus told the three parables in that chapter, about the lost sheep, the lost coin and the sinful son.

Long ago I adapted the story of the son as follows: When I arrive at heaven at long last and rejoice to be in the presence of God and of all good people, the very first person I shall see, loved and cherished by God, will be the very person in the whole world that I could not abide, could not stand. If I am bold enough to ask God, I ask what in heaven's name is that person doing in heaven? 'Either he (or she) goes or I go, but I am not about to spend eternity with that one.' Then, like the father of the Prodigal Son, God will say, 'I love that one; I love you. I am not sending him (her) away and I am not sending you away. Please stay, but I cannot make you stay. This is the Kingdom of Forgiveness, where you have arrived.' The story would be the same if it happened that I was there in heaven first, and the person I hated turned up to a great welcome afterwards. Who forgives, stays.

What enraged the Pharisees and scribes, then, was the way Jesus dealt with sinners, while at the same time claiming to bring good news from God. Jesus did not say to sinners, 'I forgive you' but he did say that 'Your sins are forgiven', meaning 'God has forgiven your sins.' Equally, he did sometimes say, 'Neither do I condemn you.' God, if anyone, is the one to condemn, but God is not condemning. God is not about condemning, God is about forgiving, so in the end the only unforgivable sin is to do with not forgiving – with refusal to forgive or refusal to be forgiven.

The enemies of Jesus were priding themselves on keeping the Law of Moses down to the last detail, but as Jesus said, they were intent on the last detail at the expense of several major requirements of the Law which they overlooked. 'We are perfect; we do not need forgiving; we do all the right things. The rest of the world is of no consequence to God, and of no consequence to us. The sick and infirm are sick and infirm because of sin, so we keep ourselves away from them. God has abandoned them and all sinners, so we may safely keep away from them as well.'

The enemies of Jesus were justifying themselves, thinking that God's approval is something to be earned by right behaviour. They did not aim to obtain forgiveness themselves since they were perfect already. They did not understand that entry into Paradise is a gift above and beyond the keeping of any rules.

What about the sin against the Holy Spirit, that can never find forgiveness (see Mark 3:29)? The Holy Spirit enables us to cry 'Abba! Father!' The Spirit opens up the whole enormous vista of being a child of God, free from taxes to God. To refuse to accept heaven as a gift, to feel one has earned Paradise and that the rest of the world has not, that surely leads to despising many others and being unwilling to share heaven with them. The Pharisees and their like were manufacturing a paradise of their own, unaware that it was not God's kingdom, because it was not the kingdom of forgiveness.

Before God there is no need for pretence: there is no need to pretend before the God who is forgiveness. With other human beings in this world we often need to hide, cover up, try to appear better than we know we are. The Pharisees apparently were given to pretending before God, and that did not endear them to Jesus: showing off at prayer, at fasting and at almsgiving to impress the general public rather than being honest and humble with God. The only virtue Jesus wanted people to excel at was forgiveness: forgive as often as you like, as often as you can, seventy times seven times every day.

Christians, of course, do not have to be faithful to all the Law of Moses, but even that part of the Law to do with the Ten Commandments is not as crucial as the law of Jesus that we be prepared to forgive one another. His new commandment was to love one another as he loved us, and his love for us includes forgiveness. God is love, and God is forgiveness, so to be like the Son of God we have to forgive, every time. The story goes that the beloved disciple John in his old age was forever repeating, 'Little children, love one another.' Today we need to hear 'Little children, forgive one another' just as often.

When the risen Jesus says to the disciples, 'If you retain the sins of any, they are retained' (see John 20:23), he could only be saying to do as he did; he is not telling them to watch out for new sins. And the only sin that Jesus ever retained was that of refusing to forgive. Jesus was angry, true enough, about the state of the temple, the people buying and selling God's favours to the highest bidder, but he did not 'retain' the situation: he cleared the lot out, and prepared to give them a new temple instead.

Most people today, apart from the Jewish community, are not immediately concerned with the Law of Moses. But today most Christians have a code of ethics, a list of things that should be done and the things that should be avoided. Other faiths and people of no faith normally have at least a mental list of actions they approve and actions they disapprove of. Everybody is at risk of refusing to forgive whoever crosses their own boundaries of the permissible. What Jesus is saying about forgiveness applies to anyone at all who has moral standards: he tells us to forgive those who transgress our personal limits of what is acceptable. To forgive is not the same as to condone, but forgiving includes a respect for the wrongdoer, and a willingness to try and understand what made the sinner sin. It also includes a willingness to admit one's own failure to live up to one's own moral standards.

What about these two kingdoms, the kingdom of Forgiveness and the kingdom of 'Pay up'? I believe that Jesus is saying that Paradise and the kingdom of heaven is the ultimate reality, and that forgiveness is the key to Paradise. In the end, nothing will last apart from the real world of forgiveness. Revenge is unreal, judging is unreal; judging one another cannot co-exist with forgiveness, so revenge and judging have to go. 'Pay up' is not just a question of money and financial debts: the demon is the insistence that everyone else should live up to my standards.

Jesus adds a safety clause, to make forgiving enemies more possible. He says to pray for our enemies, and he equates that with forgiving the enemy (Matthew 5:43-45). We can at least pray for our enemies, that they may see the error of their ways, that they may see how deeply they have hurt us, that they will not do the same to anyone else, and so on. Forgiving is not a burden, but once welcomed it is felt as a great relief, and the removal of a burden. 'I believe in the forgiveness of sins', as it says in the Apostles' Creed: my sins, your sins, everybody's sins.

The parables of Jesus are usually open to more than one meaning, depending on who hears them, and there is an appropriate meaning for the wedding garment in Matthew's version of the parable of the wedding feast (see Matthew 22:1-14). In Luke's version of the same story we hear Jesus saying that everybody in sight is to be invited to the wedding feast, from the highways and byways, whether they have a wedding garment or not (see Luke 14:21). In Matthew's version the man who was excluded was one who had no wedding garment (see Matthew 22:11-13). The conclusion has to be that the wedding garments, like kaftans, were there to be picked up and donned by the guests as they came in; the fault of the defaulter was that he did not deign to pick one up – he thought he was perfect enough already. In spiritual terms, the wedding garment equals forgiveness. God's forgiveness is there for everyone, and we only have to pick it up and wear it.

Bread, water and wine: 'wine' and the Word

In this chapter I wish to investigate the link between the wine of the Eucharist and the word 'Abba'. First of all, may I present a diagram of relationships:

body	soul	spirit
bread	water	wine
body of Christ	human life of Christ	divine life of Christ

The top line refers to what Paul thinks of as our entire being: 'May the God of peace himself sanctify you entirely; and may your spirit and soul and body be kept sound and blameless at the coming of our Lord Jesus Christ' (1 Thessalonians 5:23). The Thessalonians, as new Christians, each have a human body, a human life and a share in the divine life – as does every Christian from that day to this.

In the ceremony of the Eucharist, the three elements used in memory of Jesus are bread, water and wine. The bread will be used to become the body of Christ, the water will represent his human life, and the wine will become his divine life.

Then, before any words of consecration, there comes a powerful little prayer:

> 'By the mystery of this water and wine
> may we become sharers in the divinity of Christ
> who humbled himself to share in our humanity.'[7]

This prayer accompanies the actual mixing of the water and the wine, again before any words of consecration are spoken. The water stands for human life, the wine for divine life. Christ had divine life always, but for him to have a human body and a human life, that was new – that was the Incarnation. The little 'mixing' prayer is a prayer that Christ's divine life may eventually become operative in each communicant.

To digress a little, about the water: 'According to ancient rule some water must be mingled with the wine. This was not indeed a native Palestinian custom, but a Greek practice that was observed in Palestine in Christ's time.'[8] Early Christian writers take it for granted that the wine of the Eucharist is mixed with water – for example, Justin Martyr writing about AD 150, and Irenaeus and Cyprian writing about AD 200. Irenaeus was born in Asia Minor, spent time in Rome and was then made Bishop of Lyon, so he represents a fair section of the Christian world. Incidentally there was no shortage of water at the Last Supper: Peter and

---

7. From the English translation of The Roman Missal.
8. J. A. Jungmann, *The Mass of the Roman Rite*, One-volume edition, p.333.

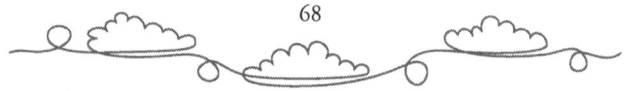

John had been directed to follow a man carrying a water container, so as to find the right address for the supper (see Luke 22:10).

Some key figures in the time of the Reformation, like Martin Luther, dropped the use of water in the Eucharist, under the impression that the water in with the wine was signifying our poor human contribution to the saving work of Christ. In fact it signifies only the human life of Christ. The divine life attended the conception and birth of Christ, and an essential truth in the Creed holds that Jesus is truly divine and truly human. The distinction between what water means and what wine means is brought out clearly in the story of the wedding feast at Cana, where Jesus changed the water into wine. There was a clear statement of intent by Jesus, that he would turn human life into divine life for us. The story dovetails perfectly with the use of wine in the Eucharist: the divine life comes from outside to transform human body and human life into a whole new being: spirit, soul and body.

One more thought about the wine before ever it is consecrated: according to the early Christian writers, wine does not fit into the list of things 'made by human hands', but wine is 'engendered by God' (Justin) and is 'from heaven' (Irenaeus). Grape juice may be thought of as 'made by human hands', but wine is something else, a gift from God. Hence wine is a suitable symbol to be transformed into the divine life of Christ.

What about 'Abba' and the wine of the Eucharist? In what way are these two vitally connected? Going back to the little 'mixing' prayer, what is the divine life that comes to share our human life? How can we identify, 'Yes, divine life is here, divine life has been given to me?' Well, one clear way to identify our share in divine life has to be the way we are now entitled to call God 'Abba, Father'. Only someone who is a child of God could ever be so familiar with God. And calling God 'Abba' makes an enormous difference to daily life: it brings self-worth, dignity, respect for others, gratitude, forgiveness, and trust. Just one little word changes the entire meaning of the world. As a mother or a father signs off a letter to each and every one of the children, saying 'All my love', so is God with each and every one of us children.

That 'one word' makes me digress again, though to something that will turn out to be very relevant. At the beginning of John's Gospel comes the enigmatic statement: 'And the Word became flesh and lived among us' (John 1:14). Volumes have been written about those words of John and about his link with ancient Greek philosophy. But to me, the Word that was made flesh was the word 'Abba!', spoken by the Second Person of the Trinity to the First Person, from all eternity. A 'Word' without content leaves me floundering: instead it has to be saying something to somebody.

The Greek philosophers got as far as seeing one perfect being who was the mountain peak of all virtues: love, duty, wisdom, beauty, any virtue. Every virtue existed in itself, in its purest form; but there had to be One being who united all perfections.

What the Greeks did not see was that there is a whole array of perfections that are reflections of beauty. What about love-in-return-for-love, what about obedience, what about admiration, what about thanks, what about adoration, what about gratitude? All of these are virtues, yet how could they co-exist in the One? Is the One to thank himself, to admire himself, to be grateful to himself, to obey and love himself?

This is where Jesus comes in as Love-in-return-for-love, as gratitude, as the one who relates to the One as Son to Father, the one who from all eternity called the One by a name that translates 'in the flesh' as 'Abba'.

There is another meaning belonging to the wine of the Eucharist that does not receive much attention. At the consecration of the wine, the words spoken over the chalice include, 'This is the chalice of my blood.' Besides the normal, obvious connection with the Passion of Christ and the shedding of his blood, there is another meaning connected with the word 'Abba'. The word 'blood' has also to do with parentage, with ancestry, with royalty. Obviously, Christ's blood is his alone, and only he is in the direct line of descent from God. But in his sharing of his parentage with us, we become in some real sense children of the royal blood, as dearly cherished as the only One. Sharing in the life of Christ at the most obvious level means calling God 'my Father'.

Again, given such links between each one of us and God, it feels less and less comfortable to be asking my loving Father for mercy, though, as ever, it feels right always to ask for forgiveness.

Perhaps I could go on to recall what happens to the bread, the water and the wine as the Mass proceeds beyond the presentation of the gifts. The words of consecration place the bread as the body of Christ; the wine mixed with water is consecrated as the blood of Christ. The words of consecration are Jesus' own words, and they separate his body (here) from his blood (there), recreating his death. He recalls to our minds the day when his body was dead and drained on the cross, and his blood with the water from his side was on the lance of the soldier or spilled on the ground.

Then, authorised by Jesus, we dare to call God our Father. Next, the bread is broken to feed however many; then a sign of peace and communion with the consecrated bread. In the meantime, a small particle of communion bread is dropped into the chalice, so that in the chalice bread, water, wine (body, blood, divine life of Christ) are reunited. Those three are reunited again in the communion under both kinds of the presiding priest, and then too in anyone else who communicates with the chalice: Christ who died now risen again.

Sacrifice and forgiveness

I have been arguing the case that when Jesus tells someone, 'Your sins are forgiven', he is stating a fact, the fact that God has already forgiven the sinner. The religious establishment of the time thought what Jesus was saying amounted to blasphemy. How did this upstart from Nazareth claim to know what God was thinking, what God was forgiving? Who did he think he was? Without even going into this sinner's case, how did he come up with such a bold statement? Is he saying that God has already forgiven all sins, past, present and in the future? That must be too soft an image of God, surely, and as such it must be eliminated, and Jesus with it.

From a Christian point of view, at the end of the story Jesus is seen to be the beloved Son of God, made man, well able to speak up for what God thinks about goodness and about sin. I have been saying that Jesus teaches us that God has already forgiven all sins, past, present and future, of the children of God. We may see as much from the parable of the Prodigal Son, where the father, like God, has forgiven both sons before ever the younger one went away, and while that one was sinning, and when he came back. There, in the one masterly story, Jesus is supplying the one image that goes with his new covenant. The father's love and the heavenly Father's love is everlasting, as a parent's love is everlasting. The love begins with the conception of the child, grows to the birth of the child, and never stops, no matter what troubles ensue.

The reckoning of what is the worst sin changes quite dramatically. As we have conjectured, God welcomes all his children into heaven, and there they can stay so long as they are willing to forgive one another. The father in the parable is happy to welcome the wastrel and is happy also to welcome the elder brother, but the elder brother may decide not to forgive, not to join the celebrations – the story is unfinished.

This situation, I would say, holds for the whole human race, not just for Christians; but hopefully Christians at least can lift up their hearts at the thought that their sins of yesterday, today and tomorrow are already forgiven. The Sacrament of Reconciliation would then be a reassurance of forgiveness already sealed and delivered: 'If you ask in prayer for forgiveness, believe that you have it already, and it will be yours' (compare Mark 11:24).

Now to the main topic of this chapter, namely to see that Christ's death on the cross was a sacrifice for the forgiveness of sins, and that this is still true, even if Jesus had been preaching everlasting forgiveness. Likewise, that the Mass is still a sacrifice, and one and the same sacrifice with that of the cross.

In the very early days of Christianity, when the disciples of Jesus gradually split off from formal Judaism, the Christians had a two-fold Sunday gathering which corresponded to the Synagogue service and the Temple worship of their former days. The Sunday Mass began with prayers, hymns, readings and a homily, similar to the pattern of a Synagogue, then on to the Eucharist which replaced the need to go to the Temple for any kind of sacrifice.

The first recorded accusation of blasphemy levelled against Jesus happened on account of him telling the paralytic let down through the roof: 'Child, your sins are forgiven'; and it was finally on a charge of blasphemy that Jesus was condemned to die. Jesus was then and always a victim, a victim of the blindness of his persecutors. This victim was slain by religious people who wanted to limit God's pleasure to themselves or to any others they approved of. Jesus still died for the forgiveness of sins, if through his death his disciples could know themselves as beloved children of God, sins or no sins. He died as a martyr to that truth; he died rather than deny what he had come to assert; he died rather than falsify the nature of God's love and forgiveness; he died rather than betray the mission of his Father.

Jesus did not aim to placate his Father, since his Father did not need placating, or appeasing, or mollifying. See the father of the Prodigal Son for Jesus' outlook on the matter. The Father was 'well pleased' with Jesus, but also well pleased to be Father to all the adopted sisters and brothers of Jesus, whom he did not condemn. 'Well pleased', like forgiveness, comes before great deeds, in the Father's manoeuvres as in the teaching methods of Jesus. Jesus was insistent on the need for his brothers and sisters to forgive one another, because failure to forgive one another was ultimately the only fault that could keep them out of heaven, the kingdom of forgiveness.

Jesus is still the Lamb of God, the Passover lamb. His dying and his blood on the cross was the means of our freedom from sin, once the truth of his mission became clear in his rising again from death. He was unblemished like the lamb in the Exodus story; he was blameless, he was without sin. Like the Servant in the Servant Songs of Isaiah, he had done no wrong, but he died to set a great multitude free.

God did not want Jesus to die, surely, but God did want the truth to be known. Jesus sacrificed himself for that, and God who is love must have known what was bound to happen to his beloved Son, his only Son. This must have been the only way universal love and forgiveness could ever get through to a deaf-blind, crippled, fallen world.

Jesus is still high priest, the only one able to go through the veil between the Holy Place and the Holy of Holies, into the presence of the Most High. Jesus, in his death, tore down the veil shrouding the divinity, so that all of us like little children may now walk freely into the presence of God our Father. God is our Saviour in the end, sending his only One to show us how to come close, whatever might seem to go badly wrong.

The new covenant of Jesus was sealed with blood like the old covenants, but this time the blood was that of Jesus, and it is the last and final covenant. 'I, your God, will be your Father, and you will be my children – there is no further need beyond that to talk about forgiveness of sins. To you, you are my beloved daughter; to you, you are my beloved son.' It cost Jesus his life blood to bring that about, Jesus who is Love-in-return-for-love.

The Mass, which records and makes real again what Jesus did on the cross, is still and always a sacrifice of thanksgiving: thanksgiving for the Father's will, thanksgiving for the life and death and rising to life again of Jesus, thanksgiving for hope and love and forgiveness in our lives. The Mass is a communion sacrifice as well, Christ offered to God and Christ shared out among us, with nobody left out. The holy cross itself is like the altar of the new covenant.

Sometimes the story of Abraham being willing to sacrifice his own son Isaac is used as a comparison with what happened between God and his only Son Jesus. First, in the Abraham story, Abraham starts out with a mistaken conscience that tells him his God wants such a sacrifice. He is willing, though presumably brokenhearted. When it comes to the holding of the knife, however, his conscience becomes clear: this barbaric custom is not something my God wants.

I do not think the story of Jesus, the cross and the Father is really in any way parallel to Abraham and Isaac. Isaac, after all, did not die, whereas Jesus did die, seeming likely to have failed in his mission. God did not want his only Son Jesus to die as any kind of sacrifice: he simply wanted Jesus to tell poor sinners that as far as God was concerned, their sins were forgiven. What happened then was so awful that at first Jesus' disciples could not make any sense of it except as sacrifice – but then, too, it dawned that the sacrifice had succeeded.

Mothers and fathers

First of all, consider this paragraph from Mark's Gospel:

> Peter began to say to him, 'Look, we have left everything and followed you.' Jesus said, 'Truly I tell you, there is no one who has left house or brothers or sisters or mother or father or children or fields, for my sake and for the sake of the good news, who will not receive a hundredfold now in this age – houses, brothers and sisters, mothers and children, and fields, with persecutions – and in the age to come eternal life. But many who are first will be last, and the last will be first.'
>
> (Mark 10:28-31)

Note that there is no promise of a hundredfold of fathers to replace the one sire left behind for the sake of the good news. Mothers, brothers, sisters, children, houses, fields, yes, all of these, but not fathers. There is no question in any of the commentaries on Mark but that the ancient manuscripts agree: 'fathers' was left out by Mark and by Jesus on purpose.

To find the reason, we have only to go to what Jesus says in Matthew's Gospel: 'And call no one your father on earth, for you have one Father – the one in heaven' (Matthew 23:9).

Another small paragraph from Mark needs to be quoted here. At the end of chapter 3:

> Then his mother and his brothers came; and standing outside, they sent to him and called him. A crowd was sitting around him; and they said to him, 'Your mother and your brothers and sisters are outside, asking for you.' And he replied, 'Who are my mother and my brothers?' And looking at those who sat around him, he said, 'Here are my mother and my brothers! Whoever does the will of God is my brother and sister and mother.'
>
> (Mark 3:31-35)

That last statement is one that should be followed up. For one thing, there is no hint at all that 'Whoever does the will of God is my father.' In addition to that, those sitting around Jesus would be men as well as women, and some at least, not necessarily elderly ladies, would be among those Jesus calls 'my mother'.

I would claim that anyone of the human race, male or female, may turn out to be a mother of Jesus, a mother of Christ. As one of the prayers in the Missal for 'giving thanks to God' puts the situation:

> 'O God, the Father of every gift,
> we confess that all we have and are comes down from you ...'[9]

---

9. From the English translation of The Roman Missal.

The only source of good, beauty, wisdom and power is the One Jesus calls his Father and ours. There is a sense in which every good person is penetrated and impregnated by the One and becomes fruitful, as in the case of a Christian bringing the life of Christ into another person where Christ was not living before. They mother 'another Christ' and not by their own power alone. There is no way any human can penetrate God and make God fruitful. The traffic is one-way and the image is sexual: God is Father, humans can be mother through the Spirit. There is a sense in which every active disciple of Jesus becomes a mother of Jesus.

This 'penetration' is always 'from outside'. When I was writing a book on the wisdom of Jesus, I listed 46 places in the Gospels where God's activity is described as 'from above' or from outside. Those who refused to recognise God at work were only blocking the way for Jesus' teaching. Here, I am sure, is the solution for those who worry about having to call God 'he' all the time: if there is only one Father, but the rest of us can aspire to mother Christ into the world, then the sexual imagery could be seen to be at balance.

There seems to be no way round the fact that Jesus called God his 'Abba', his own Father, and that he wanted us to do the same. According to the calculations of Joachim Jeremias (see Introduction for details), Mark refers to three occasions, the Q source of teachings refers to four more, Luke makes four references, Matthew gives us Jesus using 'Father' 41 times, and in John's

Gospel there are at least 100 times of using 'Father'. At least a score of times we have Jesus speaking to God as 'Father'. The only one time he did not was on the cross, 'My God, my God, why have you forsaken me?' and that one time comes between two others from the cross in which he calls on God as 'Abba'. Anyone wishing to escape as a Christian from having to call God 'Father' is in difficulties. I have been suggesting that if the males among us are more ready to be accepted as 'mother' of Christ, then the worry about 'he' for God becomes less acute.

Jesus himself did not mind taking on a female image: 'Jerusalem, Jerusalem, the city that kills the prophets and stones those who are sent to it! How often have I desired to gather your children together as a hen gathers her brood under her wings, and you were not willing!' (Matthew 23:37). Jesus is not reluctant to call himself mother hen. His children, moreover, are his children by virtue of his Father's entering him and creating 'other Christs'. Jesus never sees himself as 'father'. When he speaks to the paralytic let down through the roof and tells him, 'Son, your sins are forgiven', he is either using a colloquialism or he is christening the young man as a child of God. Similarly, when he calls the woman who had the haemorrhages 'Daughter', he was relating her to God the healer rather than to himself.

Jesus is creating a new family, with God as the one and only Father, himself as the only Son, and the rest of the world as his sisters and brothers. The renewal of the numbers in the family is brought about by a union between God and the brothers and sisters of Jesus through whom Christ is present anew in a new generation, through the mothering of the present generation. Each of us in whom Christ lives again is an adopted child of God, and what I call a first generation child of God. God is directly involved in (for instance) my being adopted, and God is not simply my ancestor, but is my 'Abba' or personal Father.

Another factor to be taken into account is that Matthew's 'only one Father' is connected with what we, in these days, would call personal conscience. Jesus is saying that we have only one Father, but the implication is that I need not follow what my father says (or my mother), nor what the clergy say, nor what the civil authorities say, if what they say is contradicted by what my own conscience says: my conscience being the voice of God. There is nothing particularly masculine about conscience, and for all I know the conscience of a woman may have a different scale of values. But I still think that, for Jesus, his Father would want men to follow their conscience, and women to follow theirs.

One boon and blessing of equating conscience with the Father's voice is that, unlike the rest of the world, we as followers of Jesus have a conscience that can forgive us if we go against it. We can be forgiven and start again. One of the greatest blessings of being a follower of the Way of Jesus is that I can start each day with yesterday already forgiven. There is one other father in the world-view of Jesus: there is the father of lies (see John 8:44). The people who were stubbornly refusing to go along with the Spirit of Jesus were, he reckoned, benighted from listening to the father of lies and denying the light. One example I have already noted, namely that which dominates the kingdom of pay-up-what-you-owe. That spirit demands that everyone pay up exactly what they owe me; that everyone keeps the same rules, civil, family, religious, as I do; that if people disobey they must be made to pay up; that the people I judge are to be judged and sentenced, and so on. This is the kingdom of darkness, and the kingdom of the unreal. I have already suggested that revenge is a non-event in God's eyes.

In contrast to the kingdom of pay-up is the kingdom of forgiveness, otherwise known as 'Freely have you received, freely give.' I have been given God's forgiveness without ever having to pay for it: so the least I can do is to pass it on.

God loves,
God sends the Spirit
to make me God's child.

> In gratitude, I wish to love in return.
> Jesus sends the Spirit to give courage.
> I love-in-return-for-love.

Why Jesus had to die

When I was studying theology in Ireland a long time ago, I was fortunate to have among my teachers a very wise old priest by the name of Johnny Hyde. One saying of his I have always remembered and treasured: it was about the character of the sacrament of baptism, character being a technical term for the reason why baptism can never be given twice, since the first time has a permanent effect. Father Hyde said, 'The character of baptism is that it gives a place at the table.' The one baptised has, from then on, his or her own place at the family table of God, which can never be given away to anyone else and which is always there awaiting the rightful occupant. Immediately there comes to mind the picture of the Prodigal Son, who comes home in trepidation but who finds his place and his welcome was never lost – his father kept his place at the table always open for his return. Such is the relationship Jesus draws and pictures between God and the sinner, a love that can stand any amount of betrayal and still make room for the lost one.

This surely was the reason why the enemies of Jesus were determined to kill him: they wanted to earn God's respect and love by their own doing, and they wanted God to go along with them in condemning anyone else who did not make the grade.

I have been writing in these pages to support the belief that God's love is unconditional. Along with that, and perhaps amounting to the same truth, I do believe that God has already forgiven all our sins, past, present and to come. If God is forgiveness, forgiveness does not change from past to present to future. Hence when Jesus sees a person ready to believe in forgiveness, he can say to the sinner, 'Your sins are forgiven' – not because Jesus says so, but simply as a fact. But who was Jesus to say so confidently what God is thinking about the sinner? Centuries later, I can say the same to a sinner, but only through what Jesus said, and through the terrible consequences he willingly suffered, to get his message accepted. Jesus did not have to die, only that he brought to a head his confrontation with his foes.

Who were the foes? Not the ordinary citizens and sinners, who found Jesus' teachings most attractive. The Pharisees as a body were distressed over Jesus' teaching. As far as they were concerned, a blind person could not read the scriptures so a blind person must be out of favour with God. A deaf person could not hear the hymns or the psalms or the sermons, so must also be out of favour with God. A paralysed person could not get to synagogue or to Jerusalem, so was limited in God's eyes. A leper was clearly cut off from society and did not belong in God's people. Sinners in general who could not keep to the Law of Moses did not belong either. Yet all these people with handicaps were the very ones that Jesus favoured, acting as if God had sent him particularly to them first of all.

The Sadducees, the high-priestly party, to some extent owed their position and their living to the Roman conquerors, and so the Sadducees were nervous of the huge popular appeal of Jesus. Jesus had thousands following him about in Galilee and up-country, and the occupying power is always nervous about possible uprisings. An uprising would be bad news for the Romans, and hence for the Sadducees.

The Zealots and the patriots would have supported Jesus and even made him king if he had been willing, but they were disappointed: that was not the sort of kingdom he came to establish. In the end, there was not much support for Jesus from the Zealots. His apostle Simon the Zealot was an ex-Zealot.

In general, the authorities and the scribes were horrified at the manoeuvre of Jesus described above in chapter three. That Jesus should start with complete forgiveness before going on to ask for improvement of life was unthinkable. Even today, there are many religious people who want to use God as a threat to make people, young and old, toe the line, and who do not accept a God who forgives first. Perhaps I should repeat once again that God is love, and divine love always leaves free the possibility of there being no return of love.

Jesus came to the climax, where his enemies were in their stronghold of Jerusalem. On his final entry into

Jerusalem, there were crowds of pilgrims from outside the city who were loud in their praises of Jesus, but once he was inside the city he was in serious danger from his enemies, who could manipulate the city-dwellers to outnumber and out-shout the disciples of Jesus and his well-wishers on a key occasion.

Jesus accepted that one of his twelve chosen apostles would betray him, and was willing enough that the trial of strength should come to pass in the Garden of Gethsemane. Jesus had a stark choice, either to run away and leave the public stage, thus leaving the sinful world still believing in God as an enemy, or else to hold to his belief and let the foes kill him for preaching God's already forgiveness. If he had run away, then I for one would never have dared to think of God as my beloved Father, my Abba. My sins were already forgiven but I would never have known it and I would never have known why.

Jesus was well aware of the prophesies regarding the Messiah, the Chosen Leader who was to come. There were other prophesies as well, predictions of triumph and glory, which he may have thought at the time would come to pass in his own human lifetime. But as his public life went on, it became clearer and clearer that the painful predictions were to be his destiny, before and on the way to his glory. There are two key lessons Jesus had to teach his disciples: God loves me though I am a sinner, and God loves me even though I am suffering through no fault of my own. In the garden Jesus was praying to his Father (and mine), 'Abba, Father, for you all things are possible; remove this cup from me; yet, not what I want, but what you want' (Mark 14:36). It was not possible, not there and then, though the time would come very soon. Jesus was in a human situation, and it had to be played through, even though God's love was never in doubt.

None of this made sense to the disciples at the time. They thought maybe Jesus had been wrong after all in his teaching of forgiveness, and that the death on the cross was also the death-knell to his picture of God as his Father, his Abba. Only little by little, or rather by a thunderclap, in a few days' time did they see the point of all this suffering. Here had been a New Covenant, the one that says from God, 'I will be true to you, even if you are untrue to me.' Even, in traditional manner, the new covenant was now sealed in the blood of a victim, and the victim was Jesus himself – not to appease God, but to assert total belief that God's forgiveness is already here. The real new need is that we learn to forgive one another.

'Father, forgive them; for they do not know what they are doing' (Luke 23:34). These are the words of Jesus as he is nailed to the cross. Oddly, we find that these words are omitted in some ancient manuscripts, though the consensus of Gospel editors leaves them in as authentic. To my mind, we have a choice: either, Jesus did not say them and some copyist invented them and put them in, or else Jesus did say them and certain copyists decided against including them. That anyone else but Jesus would dream of such a sublime dying wish strikes me as totally unlikely. If, however, Jesus did plead with his Father for the forgiveness of his murderers, who would gain by leaving the words out? One not-impossible culprit would be anyone who did not comprehend the message of Jesus about forgiveness; another possible culprit would be someone swayed by anti-Semitism. There was a lot of it about, even visible as early as the Acts of the Apostles, where Jesus' death is often blamed on the Jews, as if the fault was theirs alone. The words of Jesus on the cross are themselves clear evidence of the importance of forgiveness in the kingdom of Jesus.

Another factor to bear in mind is this: Luke, in his Gospel, gives us Jesus saying, 'Father, forgive them; for they do not know what they are doing' (23:34), and also 'Father, into your hands I commend my spirit' (23:46). The same Luke in the Acts of the Apostles gives us Stephen, the first Christian martyr, echoing the same two sentiments as he dies, this time addressing them to Jesus ascended to the right hand of God: 'Lord, do not hold this sin against them', and 'Lord Jesus, receive my spirit' (Acts 7:59, 60). There is no indication why the words asking for forgiveness should be kept for one situation but dropped for the other.

All in all, Jesus had to die or else be unfaithful to his Father's very being. He was a martyr to the truth. His Father did not desire his death, and did not need appeasing, but could not vindicate his Son this side of that Son's dying.

What only God can do

The New Testament is quite clear that the raising from the dead of Jesus is not something he achieved by himself. He was raised to life again by God, by the Father. Further, this must mean that God approved of all that Jesus stood for: the forgiveness of sins, Jesus' Sonship of the Father, Jesus' welcome to all of us mortals as sisters and brothers of himself, and adopted children of God. In the Gospels, in the Acts of the Apostles, in the letters of Paul and in the first letter of Peter, there are at least twenty statements to the effect that God raised Jesus from the dead or that Jesus was raised by God. Besides those statements mentioning God, there are at least another fifteen to say Jesus has been raised: there again God is presumed to have been the agent, since no one else in heaven or on earth could have done such a thing.

Another factor about the resurrection of Jesus had better be noticed. The accounts in the Gospels are sometimes a little confused – not remarkable really given such a divine event dropping into ordinary lives. However, there are the following thirteen items where all the accounts agree:

> That Christ died
> for our sins
> according to the scriptures.

That he was buried.

That he rose
on the third day
according to the scriptures.

That he appeared to the Eleven;
he appeared to Peter (plus message);
he appeared to many disciples at once.

Women were the first witnesses;
the tomb was empty (on the third day);
he was difficult to recognise at first.

The Scriptures predicting his death came home to the minds of Peter and the others, once they saw that his death was not the end, even though he had been well and truly buried. Later on, Peter even seems ready to understand 'rose on the third day according to the scriptures' as being prophesied in Psalm 16, verse 10: 'You will not let your Holy One experience corruption' (see Acts 2:27 and compare what Martha says in John 11:39).

The tomb was already empty on day three; this was not a piece of stage management later in the forty days. As for Jesus being hard to recognise at first, that is surely not surprising. For the most part, those who were taken by surprise ended by being totally convinced, and being willing to die for the truth of what they had seen.

I have found that one of the Rules for the Discernment of Spirits in the Spiritual Exercises of St Ignatius Loyola is a help towards understanding the nature of the Resurrection experiences.[10] Here is what Ignatius writes:

'Only God our Lord can give consolation to the soul without preceding cause: for it is the Creator's prerogative to enter the soul and leave her, and to arouse movements which draw her entirely into love of his Divine Majesty. When I say "without cause" I mean without any previous perception or understanding due to which such consolation could come about through the mediation of the person's own acts of understanding and will.'[11]

On this reckoning, only God could have given the supreme consolation of seeing Jesus alive again and well. The women on the Sunday morning were going to anoint the body of Jesus. To see him alive was completely beyond their expectation: the joy was from God alone.

The apostle John, seeing the empty tomb, understood the meaning but it was a sudden dawning given to him. The two disciples on the road to Emmaus were not using their own acts of understanding and will to create a risen Lord: indeed they were going home because their hopes were all over.

---

10. See my article *What only God can do* in The Way Supplement No 34, pp.61-69.
11. *The Spiritual Exercises of Saint Ignatius*, Ipsissima Verba, quoted by Louis J. Puhl S.J., Loyola University Press, Rules for Discernment of Spirits II. 2, quoted verbatim. 1952.

Mary Magdalene wanted to know where the body of Jesus had been taken, so she could go and anoint it. She saw Jesus and took him for the gardener, so far was she from expecting to see him. But her joy was ecstatic when she did recognise him.

Thomas was sceptical about the statements of the others that Jesus had come into the supper room on the first Sunday, but his reaction was sublime when he was convinced, saying 'My Lord and my God!' (John 20:28).

Peter is mentioned early on as being part of the entourage, but his first meeting with Jesus is not given in detail. In the boat, though, when he and six others had spent the night fishing, he leapt out and swam ashore when he realised that it was Jesus cooking breakfast. His reinstatement by Jesus on the seashore is deeply personal and touching, three commissions to match Peter's three denials.

What about Paul, the apostle born when no one expected him? There is no way he was creating for himself a risen Jesus, since he was busily persecuting the Followers of Jesus' Way, when a sudden and total conviction and consolation came to him.

The personal touches between Jesus and the witnesses are perhaps the most convincing, as well as the most endearing. Mary Magdalene must take the prize, when Jesus has only to say her name, 'Mary' and she knows him from beyond the grave. It must be the way he says it, differently from anyone else. Just a simple name, but it straddles all the way from everyday converse, through death, to a risen and indestructible life. To me it is an assurance that in the risen life we will share with Jesus, we shall also know each other by our names.

Now, some further characteristics of these 'out of the blue' experiences. They may be to do with twenty-first century thinking but they may still shed light on the Resurrection scenes. Of course, only the men and women who had been for two or three years in Jesus' company could guarantee that Jesus risen was one and the same person with Jesus of Nazareth, but all the same, present-day close encounters with Jesus can share some of the consolation.

First characteristic: that God is found to be lovely. There is not a single dissenter on that score among the women and the apostles and disciples.

Second characteristic: God is found to be real. People enjoying 'out of the blue' consolations find life with Jesus more real, not less real, than ordinary conditions.

Third characteristic: God is loving – in spite of the crucifixion. The crucifixion came about only through Jesus witnessing to the forgiveness of sins. God is love; God is forgiveness.

Fourth characteristic: God is here, my Abba, my personal Father.

Fifth characteristic: God cares about me. Each of the women, apostles and disciples enjoyed a personal encounter with Jesus risen.

A sixth characteristic runs like this: God will not forget me. God has known and loved me through every moment of my life so far, so how could he ever stop remembering me? If Jesus did not say, at the Last Supper, that 'I will never forget you', that would still be the way the hearers understood him to mean.

Seventh: God will come back this way. The total surprise, coming out of the blue and against all the odds, telling me that Jesus was here but is going away again, convinces that he will certainly come back again. He could not bring such joy and conviction from God, and then just disappear. After all, he said in many different ways that he would not leave us orphans. The clouds into which Jesus retires are, at least from a twenty-first century witness, clouds of the mind, withdrawal symptoms, but they still contain a promise that Jesus, and the glory of God, will return.

Eighth: God has something in mind for me. All the women, apostles and disciples had a new vocation, as witnesses to the Resurrection of Jesus. However they would fulfil that vocation would vary from person to person.

In general: the experience of 'out of the blue' consolations is totally unexpected, as was to see Jesus risen. It may sometimes be related to what was going on in everyday life – as with Paul who was 'kicking against the goad', not wanting to believe that Jesus might, after all, have been true to God.

Life will never be the same again. Certainly for the witnesses, life was never the same again. And indeed, life for anyone who experiences one of these 'out of the blue' consolations, life is never the same again. Sometimes a consolation of that nature is a bit like being donated a bullet-proof vest. There will be snipers wanting to shoot down such a picture of a loving God, but the witness is protected – not for life, but enough for the purpose of witnessing. The Acts of the Apostles and the history of the Church provide plenty of examples.

Such a consolation gives *a confidence that cannot be overcome in argument.* Here we need to mention that Saint Ignatius makes a difference between the moment of conviction, and the conclusions we may add by our own reasoning. The consolation is from God alone; the subsequent arguments may be our own.

Sometimes the experience is so precious that it is meant to be shared with everybody. For this one could instance the Apostle John, and his description as 'the disciple Jesus loved'. Any of us could be so overwhelmed by knowing ourselves completely loved and forgiven by Jesus. The first reaction is gratitude and worship, but then comes the thought: 'He loves me so deeply and I have done nothing to deserve such love. You, my neighbour, my friend, even you my enemy, Jesus loves you just as gratuitously. Listen to him.'

13

All sins are forgiven

Fairly clearly, in the understanding of believers, the Resurrection of Jesus is a vindication by God of all that Jesus stood for. It still leaves somewhat open the exact nature of what God is approving. I have been arguing that the key message of Jesus was forgiveness: Jesus came to save sinners, Jesus came to tell sinners they have already been forgiven; God has already forgiven all sins, past, present and future; therefore good people, the 99 sheep must get ready to forgive the sinners as God does, or they will land themselves in trouble. God is willing to forgive 77 times over, or indeed 490 times, so good people must be prepared to do the same.

Beyond this, there is the structure of God's kingdom of forgiveness. Jesus is seen to be the Son of God, since he speaks so familiarly to God as his own Father, and he is now clearly allowed to do so. He is justified also in welcoming all comers as his sisters and brothers, and assigning a baptism ceremony as the normal way of entry into the relationship with himself and with God.

I recall another image I once had, of being invited to Buckingham Palace for a Royal Garden Party. This never happened to me, but it did happen to friends of mine. So, there I am with the royal guests, and her Majesty the Queen actually comes my way and I am introduced to her. I shake the gloved hand, and am pleased that she seems to know why I have been invited there.

Now just supposing I said to her Majesty, 'Yes, thank you, Ma'am, for inviting me. But what about that gentleman over there, with the pink tie? Surely he should not be here in the company of your Majesty? I could tell you so many unsavoury things about him. And what about that lady over there in the blue bonnet? Her life leaves a lot to be desired, and she has done me personally a great deal of harm.' Well, if I said those manner of things, her Majesty might not have me thrown out on the spot, but she would certainly remember not to invite me again.

There surely is the nub of the matter. God has already forgiven everybody for everything, because we are his adopted children and for no other reason. Now, all that remains is for us to forgive one another. Perhaps we are not such 'good people' after all, since we are not yet completely and unconditionally forgiving of each other, the way God is. When all is said and done, the most vital word of Jesus to remember is 'Do not judge, and you will not be judged.'

The parable of the Prodigal Son contains all of this and is clearly crucial. The father of the sinner has already in fact forgiven his wayward son, and can hardly wait for him to return and be made welcome. The elder brother is a good man, but with possibly a fatal flaw, in that he cannot forgive the younger brother, or the father for that matter. We all like to whitewash the story of our past lives, as the elder brother did: but he overlooked his own jealousy and resentment. Jesus, of course, is elder brother to all of us Christians, and he shows us how it should be done, being just as keen as his Father to welcome the stray. Even on the cross, Jesus has no need to say 'I forgive you', but is asking his Father to do as always.

The Early Church thought: 'Yes, that was it! All sins are forgiven,' and the liberation of knowing forgiveness made a positive Christian life possible and agreeable. The manoeuvre of Jesus (forgiveness first; improvement next) seemed to be working. Yet that approach did not seem always to work, particularly with people who were still earthbound in their thinking, not really caring whether they were forgiven or not.

I would still hold that the way of Jesus is the only divine way. Even in the Trinity, the First Person loves the Second Person, the Father loves the Son, but the love-in-return has to be free. 'I will still love you, even if you do not love me in return.' The Son was not free to love, unless he was free not to love.

It is truly liberating, to know I am forgiven, when being forgiven truly matters. There is, sadly, a situation which has arisen, certainly in this country and certainly over the last hundred years, whereby a sinner who has not been to confession (the sacrament of reconciliation) to confess a serious sin feels himself to be in danger of eternal damnation if he dies before reaching a priest to confess to. That is not an imaginary situation, but one that many have found themselves in. Surely, in the interests of a happy death and palliative care, it would be better if it were known that God has already forgiven the sin, and that it is enough to be sorry.

Epilogue

And so we come to the end of our jig-saw. In the Introduction were found the outside edge pieces, the framework of the matter. In the small chapters that followed there came the pieces of the jig-saw that filled in the gaps. Here, in this last chapter, we find the last piece that was missing, to complete the picture of God's forgiveness. Besides the timeless saying of God, 'I have loved you with an everlasting love,' there comes the simple statement of faith, 'I cannot ever lose God's love: God's love is not mine to lose.' Thanks be to God.

The Key to the Kingdom

**A Bible puzzle, with the answers
chapter by chapter**

1. How can holy God keep both of two promises, namely that your unfaithful nation will be swept from the earth and from God's love (e.g. Joshua 23:15, 16), but the same holy God has loved you with an everlasting love (Jeremiah 31:3)? If the love was everlasting then it still must be everlasting today.

   Each of these promises, in one form or another, appears in one form or another in the Bible. How can they both be true? The answer is in forgiveness: everlasting love overturns the unfaithfulness. Do you agree?

2. Jesus says, 'Do not judge, and you will not be judged' (Luke 6:37). This can be understood in one of two ways: either, practise not judging other people, and then God will not judge you – or, holy God is already not judging, and if you stop judging you enter God's realm or kingdom where judging is no more.

Which of the two do you find more likely? Remember, Jesus also said, 'Whatever you ask for in prayer, believe that you have received it, and it will be yours' (Mark 11:24). Jesus also said we should forgive 77 times or 70 x 7 times, that is, every time (Matthew 18:21, 22). Surely if this is what God wants, then God will do as much and more, forgiving us our sins that many times and more?

3. Which is Jesus' way of proceeding, to ask for repentance first and then forgive, or to forgive first and only then look for improvement in the way of life?

The first would be hard to find; the second is all over the place in the Gospels, as for instance when Jesus says, 'Son, your sins are forgiven' to the young man let down through the roof (Mark 2:5) or 'Your sins are forgiven' to the woman who was a sinner gatecrashing the banquet (Luke 7:48). In fact, I believe there are no instances of Jesus ever saying 'I, Jesus, forgive your sins': with him it is always a statement that God (his Father) is the one who has forgiven the sins. Often, the simple fact of befriending a sinner is Jesus' way of indicating his Father's friendship. Do you agree?

4. 'Our Father' or 'My Father'? Which did Jesus teach first? 'My Father' and 'Abba!' for adoption and 'advocate' (Luke 11:2-4; Romans 8:14-16), or else the less personal version in Matthew 6:9?

5. No taxes for the children, including adopted children; only a voluntary contribution is called for (Matthew 17:24-27). Now that God is my Abba, life is no longer a slavery. Can you feel the difference, and can you feel huge gratitude?

6. Gifts from God come free; requests from God are voluntary. Receiving gifts is easy to do; active contribution can be difficult but is voluntary.

7. Two kingdoms or ways of living: 'Pay what you owe' as opposed to 'Forgiveness'; letting off people I disapprove of, but whom God has forgiven – most dangerous of all.

8. Water into wine – human into divine. How do I experience 'being a sharer in the divine life, partaker in the divinity?' One answer, when I can call holy God: 'Abba'.

9. Jesus on the cross was a sacrifice, but not one offered to appease God, who did not want or need appeasing. Jesus was on the cross for having been thought too generous with God's forgiveness.

10. Mothers and fathers: Sharing in the divine life, I may become sister, brother and mother of Christ Jesus; but I can never become father of Christ.

11. Why did Jesus have to die? From the very start, by saying 'Your sins are forgiven', Jesus let it be known that he knew the mind of God in the matter of forgiveness. Furthermore, he held that God has forgiven 'all the wrong people'. This could not be tolerated by godly people.

12. What only God can do: Only God can bring to the human heart a total consolation, replacing in an instant, and permanently, a deep sorrow that prevailed until then. Jesus, suddenly alive after being very much dead, was all the proof needed by the followers of the things Jesus had taught, including his teaching about forgiveness.

13. How could Jesus be so sure some stranger's sins were forgiven? Surely because he knew that all sins are forgiven, past, present and future?